RAND

Commercial Power Centers in Emerging Markets

Gregory F. Treverton, Hugh P. Levaux,
Charles Wolf, Jr.

with

Ian O. Lesser, David Robalino, Michele Zanini, Daochi Tong

National Security Research Division

Preface

This summary report is based on a considerable base of empirical research, in particular four country case studies on Mexico, Turkey, China and Indonesia. The countries were selected from among emerging economies to cover a range of regions, cultures and stages of economic growth. The authors of the cases are, for Mexico, David Robalino, with Gregory Treverton; for Turkey, Michele Zanini, with Ian Lesser; for China, Daochi Tong; and for Indonesia, Hugh Levaux. Charles Wolf, Jr. oversaw production of the last two cases, in addition to suggesting valuable cross-cutting insights throughout the project.

All these people share credit for this summary report, for the project was indeed a group enterprise. Project members came together several times to check results and test conclusions across cases. We are also grateful to the outsider reviewers of the cases—Dr. Alan Makovsky, Ambassador Edward Masters, Dr. Sidney Weintraub, Dr. K. C. Yeh, and, especially, to C. Richard Neu, who reviewed all four cases as well as a draft of this summary report. Our colleagues inside government also made many suggestions.

This project was carried out within RAND's National Security Research Division (NSRD), which does work for the U.S. Department of Defense, for other U.S. government agencies, and for other sponsoring institutions.

Contents

Figures

Tables

Summary

The influence of selected commercial power centers (CPCs) in emerging markets matters for both *what* analysts look at and *how* they view those new targets. Asia's financial crisis, which struck as this project was in its final stages, drove home that lesson in spades. All the countries examined—Mexico, Turkey, China and Indonesia—are in transition; all are attempting in varying degrees to implement what might broadly be called "market reforms"—shrinking subsidies to state-owned enterprises (SOEs), stabilizing their currencies, and opening their economies to foreign competition. In each case, the process is producing winners and losers even as it alters the rules of the economic game and thus changes the balance of power in domestic politics.

Older frames of reference for understanding those nations—dominated by single institutions, like the army, or single families, perhaps conflated with state authority, or through "deals" among a small elite—are less useful in characterizing or explaining the policy process. Policymaking and policies are becoming less the exclusive purview of governments and more the outcome of a complex process in which diverse groups participate actively, with varying degrees of influence. Thus, the emphasis on a new method using CPCs as the unit of analysis.

CPC Analysis

CPCs are defined, provisionally, as any group, combination, or coalition that seeks to influence the design and implementation of government economic policies to suit its interests. The centers need not be economic in character, but their actions must have some effect on economic policy. Thus, anti-government guerrillas in Mexico or the army in Turkey were included as power centers even though, in both cases, their primary interests are not economic.

The method evolved during the course of the work but comprised six steps: (1) Definition, (2) Collection (I), (3) Identification and Selection, (4) Collection (II), (5) Analysis, and (6) Assessment.

Step 2 involves an initial, broadly cast data collection effort using the Web, Lexis-Nexis, the Amazon bibliography, FBIS, RAND's ROBIN on-line bibliography, and other sources. Step 3 requires selecting from the set of candidate CPCs a few to be analyzed. This step requires explicit criteria to guide the selection process (for instance, sales, profits, employment, assets, liabilities, exports, imports); ownership (public, private, mixed); economic sector (consumer goods, producer goods, services); technology level (high, medium, low, dual-use). Of these, we gave pride of place to scale (sales, employment, assets, profits for business); for nonbusiness organizations—such as labor unions, or environmental groups—the relevant indicators might include membership, revenues from dues, asset balances, and the like. For both, scale was regarded as a first proxy for "clout" in influencing public policies.

Since the point of the exercise was to fashion a different perspective on the politics of emerging markets, the first cuts tended to avoid centers of interests as represented by traditional political actors, such as parties and labor unions. As the set of CPCs was refined, however, some of those were reinserted if their exclusion seemed to bias the analysis or if important power centers could not be characterized without them.

To achieve some comparability, each CPC analysis highlights the following key issues: (1) the specific policy domains on which each CPC focuses (e.g., tax policy, trade policy, opening or protection of domestic markets, national treatment for foreign investors or preferential treatment for indigenous investors); (2) the channels of influence used by each CPC and other lineal connections, foreign allies, etc.; and (3) changes and continuities over time.

Analyzing channels of influence is particularly difficult, because those channels are often murky, sometimes intentionally so: Interest groups seldom advertise their bribes of government officials and often use more oblique inducements than bribes to influence behavior. The centers can influence policy at either the *local* or the *national* level, and of one of the following types:

- formal linkages (when the linkage is established through social organizations, such as professional colleges or business associations)

- functional linkages (when a member of the power center is appointed to a public portfolio in one of the channels)

- forced linkages (when the linkage is forced by social mobilizations, such as strikes or anti-government protests)

- electoral linkages (when the center funds the political campaigns of members of the channels)

- corruptive linkages (when the center "contracts" services from the officials astride one of the channels or, less egregiously, offers shareholding to relevant government officials).

The final step should assess the effectiveness of each CPC's influence with respect to (a) specific policies it has sought to influence and (b) the relative degree of influence exercised by other, and perhaps opposed, CPCs. Reaching assessments about causation is also knotty: If a CPC's preferred policies were adopted by the government, were the center's actions decisive, irrelevant, or somewhere in between, one element in a complicated set of policy drivers? That is, did the policy result because of the center's actions, or would the same policy have resulted anyway, in which case the center is more accurately to be seen as the beneficiary of, not the lobbyist for, a particular government policy? Conversely, if the resulting outcome is uncongenial to the aims of a particular CPC, it may be unwarranted to infer that the CPC was without influence; in the absence of the CPC's influence, the policy might have been even more adverse.

Policy Mapping: Indonesia

The analysis can be summed up for each policy space of interest—and made very transparent—by scoring each CPC on the *leverage* it had and on the *effect* of the policy on it. The ordinal rankings are scaled from –5 to +5—from a total lack of leverage or total opposition, to very high leverage or very beneficial effect. Those rankings can then be displayed on a two-axis figure, with the horizontal axis representing leverage and the vertical one the effect on the CPC. See Figures S.1 and S.2.

If the CPCs cluster in the northeast quadrant, the government will be able to implement a policy with relative ease, because that policy is in the interests of the CPCs, and they have leverage to see it carried out. If the CPCs cluster in the southeast quadrant, however, trouble impends, because the policy hurts the CPCs, and they have leverage to block it. If the CPCs are scattered, the graphic suggests where opposition will arise and so where attention will need to be paid.

Events provided an opportunity to test the CPC method. The Indonesian economy was severely affected in the wake of the financial crisis that swept through Southeast Asia after July 1997. Indonesia underwent shock treatment partly instigated and closely monitored by the International Monetary Fund (IMF). For us, this was a chance to test the CPC analysis: How could the framework be applied to the financial crisis in Indonesia and the ensuing IMF-led rescue operation?

The rescue package for Indonesia was announced October 31, 1997. We evaluated the position of the four major CPCs—the Sino-Indonesians, SOEs, Suharto and his kin, and foreign investors—with respect to the four policies that were the core of the IMF package:

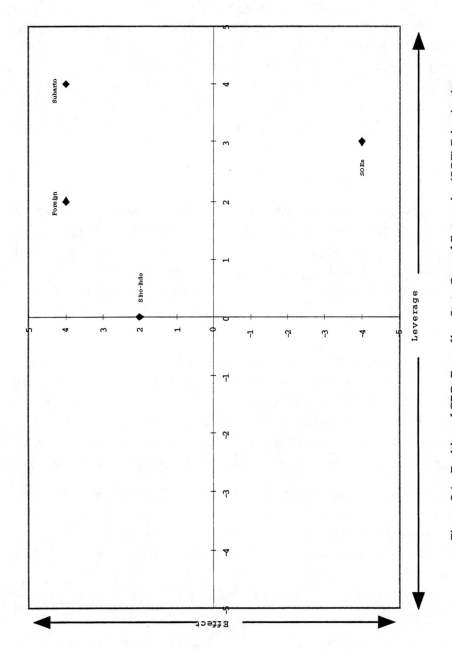

Figure S.1—Position of CPCs Regarding State-Owned Enterprise (SOE) Privatization

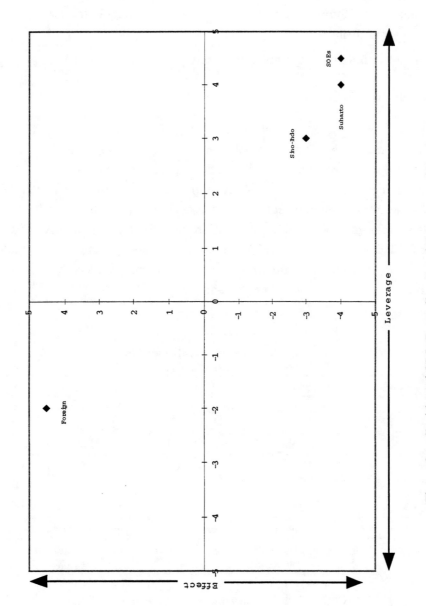

Figure S.2—Position of CPCs Regarding Equal Treatment of Foreign Investors

- Monetary policy—strict banking oversight (including potential closing of insolvent banks)

- Fiscal policy—privatization of SOEs to generate revenues and expand private enterprise

- Investment deregulation—equal treatment of foreign investors (better access to domestic distribution networks, on their own or with an Indonesian distributor of their choosing)

- Better governance—transparent government procurement rules.

Table S.1 tabulates the results.

The four policy spaces cluster in two groups. The first two, (monetary and fiscal policy), are characterized by an open policy space, with CPCs in different quadrants and with conflicting interests. In both cases, CPC-based analysis suggests that the policy can be successfully implemented and points out potential problems and sources of opposition. The last two policies (investment deregulation and governance) present a very sharp domestic-foreign dichotomy, with the foreigners in possession of little leverage. The analysis underscores that without strong, sustained pressure from the IMF and the international community, those policies will not be implemented.

Table S.1

Position of CPCs Regarding Four Policies of Interest

Policy Realm	Monetary Policy		Fiscal Policy	
Policy Issue	Strict Banking Oversight		SOE Privatization	
	Leverage of CPC on Policy	Effect of Policy on CPC	Leverage of CPC on Policy	Effect of Policy on CPC
Sino-Indonesian	3.0	–2.0	0.0	2.0
SOEs	1.0	2.0	2.0	–4.0
Suharto & Kin	3.0	–4.0	4.0	4.0
Foreign	–4.0	3.0	2.0	4.0
Policy Realm	Investment Deregulation		Enhancement of Governance	
Policy Issue	Equal Treatment of Foreign Investors		Transparent Government Procurement Rules	
	Leverage of CPC on Policy	Effect of Policy on CPC	Leverage of CPC on Policy	Effect of Policy on CPC
Sino-Indonesian	3.0	–3.0	4.5	–3.0
SOEs	4.5	–4.0	5.0	–4.0
Suharto & Kin	4.0	–4.0	4.5	–4.5
Foreign	–2.0	4.5	–2.0	4.0

The CPC-based framework of analysis is rooted in commercial interest, broadly defined, and so must be applied with considerable art to capture strictly political considerations. For instance, the Indonesian government decided not to raise the prices of staple goods, which are subsidized. The commodity import agency, BULOG, retained the responsibility to stabilize supplies and prices for rice and refined sugar. The reason probably was straightforwardly political: The president recognized that, if prices were decontrolled, they would rise sharply given the country's long and continuing drought. And that could well result in riots.

Those purely political considerations would not be easily captured by the CPC-based analysis, but, provocatively, that analysis would have suggested a similar policy outcome for a different reason. It was very much in the interest of Bogasari Flour Mills (part of the Salim group, the largest—Sino-Indonesian—conglomerate in Indonesia) to maintain BULOG's regulatory control over the import and distribution of wheat. Thus, CPC analysis would probably have predicted no change in the regulatory environment for wheat import, milling, and distribution. In the end, the IMF package replaced the import monopoly with a 10 percent tariff rate.

CPC-based analysis provides interesting insights into economic policymaking in an emerging market like Indonesia's and a very transparent way to display and discuss judgments. It provides a more micro view of the economy, producing insights into which policies are most likely to be successfully implemented. Yet it maintains a high-enough level of aggregation not to require the in-depth analysis of every industry or particular actor that may be affected by a proposed reform measure. It makes trade-off analyses explicit and helps both analysts and the policymakers think through the political cost associated with a policy option, and so helps them make better decisions.

Looking Across the Cases

To look across the cases, the power centers can usefully be grouped by relative effectiveness, high, medium, or low (Tables S.2–S.4). (This judgment is relative, for the centers were selected because their influence was notable.) At the same time, their primary channels of influence can be noted, along with whether their clout is increasing or diminishing.

This ranking suggests a number of observations:

- The high-effectiveness grouping includes both "old" and "new" power centers, both SOEs and exporters. The same is true for the low-effectiveness

Table S.2

**Centers of High Effectiveness, with Channel of Impact
and Dynamic of Influence**

Country	Center	Channel	Dynamic of Influence
Mexico	Manufactured and mining exporters	Electoral/ functional	Increasing
Turkey	Military	Formal/ functional	Increasing
China	Village and townships & enterprises	Formal/ functional	Increasing
	State-owned enterprises	Functional	Decreasing
Indonesia	Suharto and kin	Functional/ perhaps corruptive	Increasing
	Foreign investment	Forced/ formal	Increasing
	Sino-Indonesian	Formal/ functional/ corruptive?	Increasing

Table S.3

**Centers of Medium Effectiveness, with Channel of Impact
and Dynamic of Influence**

Country	Center	Channel	Dynamic of Influence
Mexico	Landowners of the north	Formal/ functional	Stagnant
Turkey	Islamists, MUSIAD	Formal and possibly corruptive	Decreasing-short run
	Secular holding companies, and USIAD	Formal/ functional	Increasing
	Unions	Forced/ formal	Decreasing
China	"Princelings" enterprises	Functional/ perhaps corruptive	Decreasing
	PLA-related industry	Formal/ functional	Decreasing
Indonesia	State-owned enterprises	Functional/ formal	Stable to receding

Table S.4

Centers of Low Effectiveness, with Channel of Impact and Dynamic of Influence

Country	Center	Channel	Dynamic of Influence
Mexico	Indians and the EZLN	Forced	Decreasing
China	Foreign-owned enterprises	Formal	Increasing

grouping. The dynamic of influence does, however, mostly point in the expected direction: Old centers, such as SOEs or armies, are declining in influence, while newer ones, such as exporters or foreign investors, are increasing. The exceptions reflect particular circumstances—for instance, the military's role in Turkey.

- The countries are, as a group, still very much in transition, both economically and politically. And they vary considerably. All retain quite centralized, administratively guided state apparatuses; for instance, in none, with the partial exception of Mexico, are legislatures of much importance, and competitive party systems are not yet sufficiently developed to make electoral channels of influence very visible.

- Mexico is the furthest along on the political path, though not the economic; China is the least, with Indonesia and Turkey somewhere in between. China and its power centers were hard to characterize, for its decentralization, perhaps more *de facto* than *de jure*, is striking in economic terms, but the country is far from politically plural, at least by western standards.

- Indeed, the analysis raises intriguing questions about China's direction. Put starkly, will China move toward a *chaebol*-like system or a truly open economy? It is worth noting, though, that there is no necessary connection between a high degree of agglomeration in industrial organization internally and closedness to foreigners externally. Japan's *keiretsu* did combine the two, though there was fierce competition at home. Given the geography and heterogeneity relative to Japan, China is unlikely to mimic Japan's MITI. At worst, it could wind up with a degraded Japanese system, with large conglomerates that were not very competitive internally but remained closed to outsiders.

- Identifying channels of influence was the trickiest part of the project. We expected there would be systematic change in channels of influence across countries. Logically, as economies emerge and political systems develop, there should be movement away from opaque, informal, especially "corruptive," forms of influence toward more regular, institutional, and transparent ones. The distinction might be thought of between *particularist* forms of influence highly dependent on personal connections and more *institutionalized* forms of systematic lobbying aimed at broader influence over policy. The ranking does hint at such a pattern.

- Finally, for intelligence, the logical focus of concentration is those power centers that are both *opaque* and *important*. That would suggest attention to the Turkish military and, secondarily, to the Islamist and MUSIAD; to China's village and township enterprises and, still, to SOEs; and to Suharto and his circle and to the Sino-Indonesians.

Glossary

CNPR	National Confederation of Rural Property Owners [Mexico]
CPC	Commercial power center
CTM	Confederación de Trabajadores de México
DEIK	Foreign Economic Relations Board [Turkey]
DIE	defense industry enterprise
EU	European Union
EZLN	Ejército Zapatista de Liberación Nacional [Mexico]
FBIS	Foreign Broadcast Information Service
FDI	Foreign direct investment
FIE	Foreign-investment enterprise
GDP	Gross domestic product
IMF	International Monetary Fund
IPR	intellectual property rights
MITI	Ministry of International Trade and Industry [Japan]
MUSIAD	Independent businessmen's Association [Islamic; Turkey]
NAFTA	North American Free Trade Agreement
NTB	Nontarrif barrier
PLA	Peoples Liberation Army [China]
PRI	Partido Revolucionario Institucional [Mexico]
SEE	State economic enterprises
SOE	State-owned enterprises
TB	Tarrif barrier
TUSIAD	Turkish Industrialists' and Businessmen's Association
VTEs	Village and township enterprises
WTO	World Trade Organization

1. Introduction

This is the summary report of an exploratory effort to frame the influence of commercial power centers (CPCs) in selected emerging markets—Mexico, Turkey, Indonesia, and China. Given the interest in methodology, it is divided into three parts: The first defines power centers and outlines a kind of "how to" manual for assessing them; the last looks across the four cases, seeking comparative insights and pointers for intelligence. The second section tests the results of the Indonesia case on a subsequent policy puzzle, asking how the earlier work on power centers will help frame that later puzzle. Summary results from all four cases are in the appendix, and the more detailed case studies are available.

The topic is crucial because, as emerging economies pursue the transition toward open markets (or seek to delay or even reverse it), their politics are transforming. Policymaking and policies become less the exclusive purview of governments and more the outcome of a complex process in which diverse groups participate actively, with varying degrees of influence. Older frames of reference for understanding those nations were dominated by single institutions, such as the army, or single families, perhaps conflated with state authority, or through "deals" among a small elite. Now, that frame of reference is becoming less accurate and less useful in characterizing and explaining the policy process.

The frame needs to be broadened in terms both of *what* intelligence looks at and of *how* it views those new targets. In particular, as the economies open and grow, old centers of power will fade and new ones will arise. As important, because all of the emerging economies are also undergoing—to one degree or another—a related process of political opening, the nature of their politics is also changing. Thus, it is appropriate to focus both on the nature of those changes and, specifically, on the forms of influence particular power centers employ. We sought both to identify new clusters of influence on economic policy and to compare them with old points of influence, seeking in the process a framework to help us understand the political changes driven by economic transformations across countries.

In the Marxist tradition, the hypothesis about links between centers of economic power and the government is pushed to the extreme; the government is in fact nothing more than the creature of the centers. In the major industrial democracies, by contrast, links between private power and public policy, while hardly above suspicion, are a tradition of longstanding and take place within developed political structures and more-or-less established rules about acceptable practices. "Lobbying" is sometimes criticized but widely practiced, generally transparent, and usually understood to be a legitimate form of political activity in a democracy. The task for this project was to understand the relationship between power centers and policy in particular countries and to ask how it varies across countries that are emerging economically but in different stages of political development.

2. Defining Terms and Assessing Power Centers

CPCs are defined, provisionally, as any group, combination, or coalition that seeks to influence the design and implementation of government economic policies to suit its interest. The centers need not be economic in character but must have some effect by their actions on economic policy. Thus, anti-government guerrillas in Mexico or the army in Turkey were included as power centers even though in both cases their primary interests were not economic. It may be worth distinguishing those centers whose character and objectives are principally economic from those whose objectives are noneconomic but whose actions have economic effects, either intended or inadvertently realized.

The methodology described below evolved, to a considerable extent, during the course of the project, rather than having preceded the onset of that work. This process is reflected in the diversity of the four emerging market case studies. Notwithstanding numerous aspects that the case studies have in common, their diversity owes both to the adaptation of the methodology to the special circumstances of each country, as well as to the evolution of the methodology during the course of the work.

The methodology comprises six related steps: (1) Definition, (2) Collection (I), (3) Identification and Selection, (4) Collection (II), (5) Analysis, (6) Assessment.

Definition

Given the definition of CPCs, they are thus "rent seeking" entities, whose aim is to initiate or modify government policies in ways that will enhance the profitability and/or other objectives of the rent-seekers or that will avoid or diminish risks to these objectives. This step broadly defines the universe to be analyzed.

Collection (I)

The second step involves an initial, broadly cast data-collection effort using the Web, Lexis-Nexis, the Amazon bibliography, FBIS, RAND's ROBIN on-line bibliography, and other sources to assemble information on both business and nonbusiness organizations that seem to exemplify the universe described in step 1, above. The information "dump" to be assembled includes indicators of scale (e.g., sales, profits, employment, assets, liabilities, exports, imports); ownership (public, private, mixed); economic sector (consumer goods, producer goods, services); technology level (high, medium, low, dual-use); etc.

Identification and Selection

Among the set of candidate CPCs, a salient subset should be selected for analysis. This step requires explicit criteria to guide the selection process. Among the several dimensions (characteristics) noted above, we suggest that the principal one should be scale—that is, the size of the selected CPC as proxied by its sales, employment, assets, profits, etc. For nonbusiness organizations—such as labor unions or environmental groups—the relevant indicators might include membership, revenues from dues, asset balances, etc.

The relevance of economic size or scale as the primary criterion for selecting among candidate CPCs is that this is probably a reasonable proxy for current and/or potential "clout" in influencing public policies. For example, the sales and profits of a CPC group will affect the attitudes and behavior of policymakers by affecting tax revenues garnered by governments, and/or through the resources they enable the group to deploy in legal or extralegal ways to lobby for or otherwise influence public policies.

In addition to this primary criterion to guide identification and selection of a subset of CPCs for detailed analysis, it may be appropriate to invoke one or more of the other characteristics of CPCs mentioned in step 3, above, to obtain greater breadth and diversity of coverage—for example, across sectors or regions of the economy, among differing technological levels, and between domestic and international economic activities. In more detail, the dimensions are as follows:

- *Scale*: What is the volume of sales, profits, employment, assets, and liabilities, and how have these changed over time? If it is not an economic unit, what other measures of its size are relevant?

- *Economic Sector:* What part of the economy? Does the center produce consumer or investment goods, services, or what?

- *Internal or External:* Does it engage in purely domestic activities, or does it import and export?

- *Ownership:* Is it privately owned, publicly owned, or mixed? Is it a foreign subsidiary?

- *Technology:* What *levels* and *types* of technology are embodied in the center's activities? And is the technology dual-use—that is, with fairly direct military application?

- *Region and/or Ethnic Identity:* In what region or ethnic community is the center rooted, and how important is this identity?

- *Institutional Lineage:* What is the provenance of the center—the military, state-owned enterprise (SOE), new entrepreneurs, and so on?

Since the point of the exercise was to fashion a different perspective on the politics of emerging markets, the first cuts tended to avoid centers of interests as represented in traditional political actors, such as parties and labor unions. As the set of CPCs was refined, however, some of those were reinserted if their exclusion seemed to bias the analysis or if important power centers could not be characterized without them.

Collection (II)

Step 4 requires digging more deeply for relevant data relating to the subset of CPCs selected for analysis. This involves both recourse to additional data sources (e.g., interviews with members of the corresponding CPC, or perhaps its adversaries), tracking of the CPCs' recent time trends with respect to the criteria used in step 3, and assembling more information from the same sources used in step 2.

Analysis

It is likely, and indeed appropriate, that the analysis of CPCs in particular emerging market countries will exhibit some degree of diversity and noncomparability because of special circumstances prevailing in each country. Nevertheless, an effort should be made to assure ample commonality in the content of each country analysis. Without such commonality, comparing across countries and among CPCs will be precluded, and the utility of the resulting product for policymakers in the United States will be less.

Toward this end, each CPC analysis in each emerging market should highlight the following key issues: (1) the specific policy domains on which each CPC focuses (e.g., tax policy, trade policy, opening or protection of domestic markets, national treatment for foreign investors or preferential treatment for indigenous investors); (2) the channels of influence used by each CPC and other lineal connections, foreign allies, etc.; and (3) changes and continuities over time.

Assessing channels of influence is particularly difficult, because CPCs may have reason to hide particular channels that might be of most interest. Through which forms or channels of influence has a CPC acted—family, clan, political parties, and so on? A longer listing of potential forms of influence would include campaign funding, open or covert; mobilizing voters; bribery; threats or promises about new businesses, scale of operations, or moving businesses or production; helping the government; and the international community, especially creditors.

Slightly more formally, the centers can influence policy through the three main governmental channels: executive, legislative, and judicial. To do so, the center needs to establish some linkage to the channel, at either the *local* or the *national* level, and of one of the following *types:*

- formal linkages (when the linkage is established through social organizations, such as professional colleges, or business associations)

- functional linkages (when a member of the power center is appointed to a public portfolio in one of the channels)

- forced linkages (when the linkage is forced by social mobilizations, such as strikes or anti-government protests)

- electoral linkages (when the center funds the political campaigns of members of the channels)

- corruptive linkages (when the center "contracts" services from the officials astride one of the channels or, less egregiously, offers shareholding to relevant government officials).

Assessment

Based on the foregoing steps, the final step should assess the effectiveness of each CPC's influence, or attempted influence, with respect to (a) specific policies (such as those referred to in the preceding step 1) that the CPC has sought to influence and (b) the relative degree of influence exercised by other, and perhaps opposed, CPCs.

Clearly, this assessment, however it may be formally approached, represents a conceptually challenging task. Many other factors—political, economic, external as well as internal—affect policy formulation and implementation besides the influence exercised by CPCs. Channels of influence are often murky, sometimes intentionally so: Interest groups seldom advertise their bribes of government officials and often use more oblique inducements than bribes to influence behavior.

Reaching conclusions about causation is also knotty: If a CPC's preferred policies were adopted by the government, were the center's actions decisive or irrelevant, or somewhere in between, one element in a complicated set of policy drivers? That is, did the policy result because of the center's actions, or would the same policy have resulted anyway, in which case the center is more accurately to be seen as the beneficiary of, not the lobbyist for, a particular government policy? Conversely, if the resulting outcome is uncongenial to the aims of a particular CPC, it may be unwarranted to infer that the CPC was without influence; in the absence of the CPC's influence, the policy might have been even more adverse.

In light of these formidable obstacles, it is important to be as explicit as possible in trying to assess the role and effectiveness of CPCs in the matrix of policymaking in emerging market countries by explicating whether and how a particular CPC did or did not account for an ensuing result.

As a hypothesis, the power centers' success in influencing the design of public policy might be thought to depend on four main factors:

1. The degree of acceptance or resistance that the policy receives from other centers, business, and nonbusiness organizations

2. The political power of the center (that is, the size of its social base and its power to mobilize large population groups)

3. The economic power of the center (that is, its importance as a contributor to growth and employment), including, as a special particular, the linkages the center has established with foreign business and finance

4. The type of linkages that the center has managed to establish with high-level government policy.

The relationship between power centers and government policy can be understood, in economic language, as that of principal and agent. Sometimes, as the center lobbies government for its preferred policies, the center can be conceived as the principal and the government as the agent. At other times, though, the roles are reversed: the government will seek to implement a change in policy by advantaging (or suppressing) a center. Mistargeting and unintended consequences may ensue; in particular, a change in policy taken for reasons having little to do with a center's interests, much less its activities, may still rebound to its benefit. Figure 2.1 displays these multifaceted interactions.

8

Each of the four cases sums its analysis through broader statements about the interaction of economy, polity, and interest group activity—what might be called the *policy and business culture*. That culture ranges from *attributes of the country as a whole*—for instance, the type of government (democratic, authoritarian), degree of public participation, role of ethnic minorities, government stability, transition from communism, and the like—to *more specific aspects of the business culture*—attitudes toward private enterprise or entrepreneurship, traditions of ownership (family versus public), traditions of collusion or cartelization, and the like.

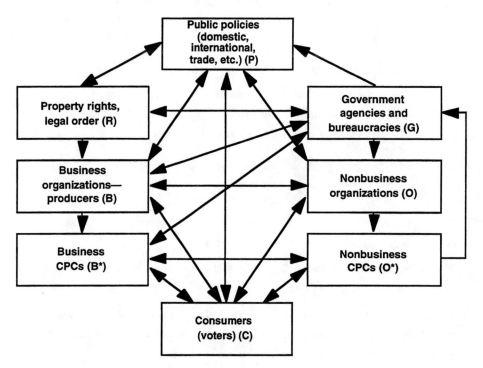

SOURCE: Provided by Charles Wolf, Jr.

Figure 2.1—Market Capitalism

3. The Vulnerability of Emerging Power Centers

All the markets we examined are in transition; all were attempting in varying degrees to implement what broadly might be called "market reforms"— shrinking subsidies to SOEs, stabilizing their currencies, and opening their economies to foreign competition. In each case, the process is producing winners and losers even as it alters the rules of the economic game and thus changes the balance of power in domestic politics.

It should be underscored that the creation of new interest groups in emerging markets, along with the concomitant demise of some older centers of power, is conspicuous in those nations because it is new. The processes, if they are novel, are so only because of where they are occurring. In contrast, in mature and "emerged" economies, such as that of the United States, economic interest groups, while sometimes criticized, are so familiar as to be taken for granted.

CPCs in the United States consist of both business organizations (such as the National Association of Manufacturers [NAM], the American Petroleum Institute, the American Bankers Association, and the Association of Home Builders) and of "nonbusiness" organizations (such as those representing labor unions, the elderly, physicians, attorneys, consumer groups, and the environment). Their actions generally take place within a relatively stable framework of economic, legal, and social institutions. For example, the Directory of Washington Representatives, *Who Does What for Whom in the Nation's Capital* (1984) lists over 8,000 organizations that either maintain Washington offices or retain someone else (e.g., law firms) to represent their interests. These include hundreds of large organizations, each with more than two-dozen staff members and multimillion-dollar budgets (e.g., AFL-CIO, the American Association of Retired Persons, National Realtors, Home Builders, Defense Industries, the American Medical Association, and the American Bar Association), and thousands of medium-sized and smaller ones. The commercial interests represented by these power centers include all industries (e.g., financial services, construction, fuels, chemicals, automotive supplies, dairy products, electronics, and computers), as well as innumerable regional and demographic groups.

Most of these "power centers" have been operating for at least several decades. As a result, they have acquired the experience and precedents of moving in well-established paths of influence in the executive and legislative corridors of both national and state governments. These centers are closely connected with networks that keep them informed about possible policy changes that may affect their interests and that they may therefore seek to influence. The centers are no less likely to try to initiate favorable policy changes than they are to influence changes that otherwise impend.

In the emerging market economies, the emergent power centers usually lack the sources of support that are available in the advanced economies. Consequently, lacking these anchors, or lacking rudders to help navigate the unfamiliar waters roiled both by external competition and internal flux, emergent power centers often reach out to the relatively limited sources of support available to them. Among these sources, those that typically exist in these economies include the military establishment; members, families, and friends of the national political leadership; provincial and local governing bodies; and foreign investors and foreign businesses, including in the Asian region those of the overseas Chinese. It is therefore not surprising that, both in China and Indonesia, the principal power centers can be identified and classified in terms of their association with one or more of these four sources of support.

In sum, power centers in emerging market economies tend to be more conspicuous because they are relatively new and also, in some cases, because they loom larger relative to the economy as a whole than they do in mature and advanced market economies. In the latter, the visibility of power centers is reduced because they are so familiar and have been around for so long that they tend simply to be taken for granted. Because power centers are so rife in the advanced economies, they may paradoxically no longer constitute anything that can be accurately referred to as a power "center." Perhaps they are more akin to electrons circling a nucleus containing various levels of government, the political party structure, the public, and a multiplicity of other particles that populate the political process.

By contrast, power centers in emerging markets are, almost by definition, fragile. Because the conditions in which they act are changing so rapidly, they are vulnerable. To be sure, the balance of power among centers in mature economies changes, but the process is usually gradual. Deregulation over a generation in the United States, for instance, has meant that groups that formerly lobbied for particular regulatory outcomes either need not or cannot do so any longer.

Power centers in emerging market economies are, and their leaderships understandably view themselves as, vulnerable to rapidly changing internal and external environments over which they have limited control. This attitude arises because the power centers of these economies are relatively new, inexperienced, and unprecedented. They are immersed in economic and social structures undergoing rapid change in unfamiliar and uncertain directions. Even seemingly large and powerful centers—like the Lippo, Astra, and Dharmala groups in Indonesia; the Sukri and Saha groups in Thailand; the Mou and Tung groups in China; and the Berjaya and Hong Leong groups in Malaysia— experience this insecurity to an extent that varies among them, as well as over time. An instructive case in point is provided by the prominent possibility that the formerly large, affluent, and seemingly powerful Mou group in China may be on the verge of collapse and dismemberment.

4. Applying CPC Analysis to Indonesia

Events provided an opportunity to test the CPC method. The Indonesian economy was severely affected in the wake of the financial crisis that swept through Southeast Asia after July 1997. Indonesia underwent shock treatment partly instigated and closely monitored by the IMF. Articles, editorials, and commentaries were published daily on the causes and consequences of the economic turmoil that ravaged ASEAN economies in those four months. The crisis was analyzed using various prisms or models—some focusing on the role of the central government, others on corruption, others on the role of international capital flows, and so on.

For us, this was a chance to test the CPC analysis: How could the framework be applied to the financial crisis in Indonesia and the ensuing IMF-led rescue operation? That is the task of this section, after outlining the crises and the main policy and reform measures (the policy package) agreed upon between the Indonesian government and the IMF. That task is an implicit test of how relevant CPC-based analysis is for other emerging markets.

Foreign investors and policymakers around the world rely on the annual World Bank report to gauge the progress of Indonesia's economy. The 1997 report, published on May 30, 1997, expressed guarded optimism. Looking at 1996, the fundamentals looked good: 7.8 percent GDP growth, inflation under control at 6.6 percent (down from 9.4 percent in 1995), and "increasingly buoyant" foreign and domestic direct investment, in the words of the bank. Yet, "despite this strong performance, significant risks remain," said the report.

Table 4.1. shows a synopsis of these risks. These factors, warned the bank, could further worsen if problems in other east Asian economies spilled over into Indonesia. Eerily, the bank concluded: "These factors, *inter alia*, risk a reversal of capital inflows, a risk that is magnified by Indonesia's large external debt and the increasing sensitivity of global capital flows to changes in indicators."[1]

Currency turmoil ignited southeast Asia when Thai authorities decided, July 2, 1997, not to defend the baht and allow it to plummet against the dollar and the Japanese yen. The speculative moves against the Thai baht quickly spread to

---

[1] World Bank, "Indonesia—Sustaining High Growth with Equity," May 30, 1997, p. xxi.

Table 4.1

List of "Significant Risks" Identified by the World Bank, May 1997

Domestic Factors	International Factors
High core inflation and key administrated prices (energy and foodstuff) not raised for a long period	Widening current account deficit, despite high international oil prices
Lost momentum on deregulation	Noticeable slowdown in non-oil exports
Weak banking sector with exposure to property market on the rise	Rapidly increasing private external debt

SOURCE: World Bank, *Indonesia—Sustaining High Growth with Equity*, May 30, 1997, p. xxi.

Indonesia. Between July 9, when pressure on the Indonesian rupiah began, and October 9, when Indonesia officially asked for IMF help, the Indonesian currency was down by almost 35 percent against the U.S. dollar, while the Jakarta stock market dropped by 40 percent in capitalization. Interim measures—the floating of the rupiah, strict tightening of liquidity and delays in $37 billion of infrastructure projects—failed to halt the slide.[2] Even if the market "overshot,"[3] the crisis revealed structural deficiencies in the Indonesian economy that compelled Indonesia to ask officially for the assistance of the international community.

The arrival in Jakarta of an IMF team calmed nervous investors. The team started work with the Indonesian delegation, headed by Widjojo Nitisastro, the 70-year old doyen of Indonesia's market-oriented economic advisors—the so-called Berkeley mafia. Nitisastro was widely regarded as the architect of Indonesia's economic development. He was not a cabinet member but was a very close and trusted advisor of the Indonesian president. The mission of the team was first to stop the ongoing crisis and, second, to put together a plan of action to address structural deficiencies in the Indonesian economy.

The rescue package for Indonesia was announced by the Indonesian government in a statement issued October 31, 1997. It was followed immediately by commending words from, among others, Michel Camdessus, the managing director of the IMF, and U.S. Treasury Secretary Robert E. Rubin.[4] On November 5, the Indonesian government and the IMF provided details about the rescue

---

[2]Peel Quentin and Thoenes Sander, "Regime tarnished by man-made calamities," in *Survey on Indonesia*, published by the London *Financial Times*, November 24, 1997, p. 13.

[3]See series of articles in the *Survey on Indonesia*, pp. 13–16.

[4]See "Camdessus Commends Indonesian Actions," *IMF News Brief* No. 97/22, October 31, 1997; and "Statement by Treasury Secretary Robert E. Rubin," *News release of Treasury Department*, October 31, 1997.

package.[5] The fund provided, *ex post*, its analysis of the structural weaknesses of Indonesia's economy and spelled out the medium-term policy strategy, with particular emphasis on reform of the financial sector and structural policies.

In discussing the background to the crisis, the IMF identified the same underlying structural weaknesses as the World Bank did in its May 30 report, though the former omitted the "high core inflation and key administrated prices (energy and foodstuff) not raised for a long period" (see Table 4.2).[6] The medium-term (three-year) policy package proposed by the Indonesian government and approved by the IMF had three main dimensions; the laser focus on the financial sector was unusual in IMF packages:

- Implement tight fiscal and monetary policies, designed to stabilize financial conditions and shrink the current account deficit

- Restore the health of the financial sector, including closing unviable banks

Table 4.2

Position of CPCs Regarding Four Policies of Interest

Policy Realm	Monetary Policy		Fiscal Policy	
Policy Issue	Strict Banking Oversight		SOE Privatization	
	Leverage of CPC on Policy	Effect of Policy on CPC	Leverage of CPC on Policy	Effect of Policy on CPC
Sino-Indonesian	3.0	−2.0	0.0	2.0
SOEs	1.0	2.0	2.0	−4.0
Suharto & Kin	3.0	−4.0	4.0	4.0
Foreign	−4.0	3.0	2.0	4.0
Policy Realm	Investment Deregulation		Enhancement of Governance	
Policy Issue	Equal Treatment of Foreign Investors		Transparent Government Procurement Rules	
	Leverage of CPC on Policy	Effect of Policy on CPC	Leverage of CPC on Policy	Effect of Policy on CPC
Sino-Indonesian	3.0	−3.0	4.5	−3.0
SOEs	4.5	−4.0	5.0	−4.0
Suharto & Kin	4.0	−4.0	4.5	−4.5
Foreign	−2.0	4.5	−2.0	4.0

---

[5]"IMF Approves Stand-by Credit for Indonesia," *IMF News Brief* No. 97/50, November 5, 1997.

[6]For discussion of these structural weaknesses, see "IMF Approves Stand-By Credit for Indonesia," op. cit.

- Implement structural reforms, including liberalizing foreign trade and investment, dismantling domestic monopolies, allowing greater private sector participation in the provision of infrastructure, and expanding privatization.[7]

This list of objectives is impressive, if familiar, and would undoubtedly improve the "national efficiency, economic endurance, and global competitiveness" of the Indonesian economy, as mentioned in the Indonesian government's statement of October 31, 1997.[8] Some measures, such as closing sixteen insolvent banks, were immediate, while others, such as guidelines for more transparent regulations of public procurement, were promised by the end of 1997. Yet many of the specific measures were to be phased in over several years—some tariff reductions would take effect only in 2003—and most were yet to be crafted. Moreover, the pace of reform would also be affected by Indonesia's growth rate. If Indonesia were somehow to return rapidly to economic boom years, pressure for reform would possibly subside as investors' confidence returned. Indonesia's promises of 1997 might be the substance of several World Bank and IMF reports but not much more—at least not before the next crisis.

To test the CPC analysis, we evaluated the position of the four major CPCs—the Sino-Indonesians, SOEs, Suharto and his kin, and foreign investors—with respect to the four policies that are the core of the IMF package:

- Monetary policy—strict banking oversight (including potential closing of insolvent banks)

- Fiscal policy—privatization of SOEs to generate revenues and expand private enterprise

- Investment deregulation—equal treatment of foreign investors (better access to domestic distribution networks, on their own or with an Indonesian distributor of their choosing)

- Better governance—transparent government procurement rules.[9]

The position of CPCs will weigh on the chances that the reform measures will be implemented. Some very important interests for CPCs are at stake. That much was exemplified by the public outburst of the president's second son, Bambang,

---

[7]The wording of these objectives is taken, almost verbatim, from "IMF Approves Stand-By Credit for Indonesia," op. cit.

[8]"Communications from the U.S. Embassy in Jakarta," addressed to Department of the Treasury and Department of Commerce, November 3, 1997.

[9]For details about the specifics of each policy, see "Communications from the U.S. Embassy in Jakarta," op. cit.

after the closing of the Bank Andromeda, of which he was a principal shareholder.

The CPC analysis can be schematically represented with a two-axis figure, as in Figures 4.1 through 4.4. Each figure represents a policy space of interest—for example, trade deregulation or privatization. The horizontal axis measures the *leverage* a CPC has on the given policy; while the vertical axis represents the *effect* of the policy on the CPCs. The figure can be used to represent a situation with respect to an existing policy or with respect to a proposed policy change. The ranking is ordinal and, for convenience, was scaled from -5 to +5. The analyst or the policymaker can rely on the mapping of the policy space (1) to evaluate the relative position of the CPCs; (2) to decide whether to implement the policy; and (3) to assess the likelihood of success of the policy.

On the *leverage* (horizontal) axis, a high positive value signifies a high CPC ability either to have a preferred policy implemented or otherwise to block or derail the policy. A low negative value, in contrast, indicates no leverage to have the policy implemented (or to oppose it). The scale ranges from –5 to +5, from total lack of leverage to very high leverage, with zero representing a neutral position. The vertical axis represents the *effect* of the policy on the CPCs. The effect of a policy can be positive or negative. This effect is not only pecuniary but also can incorporate, for example, bureaucratic control (for ministries regulating SOEs) or position in society (for the Sino-Indonesians). Effect broadly defined becomes then a gauge of the *view* of the CPC on the policy: Positive indicates support for the policy, while negative effect indicates opposition. The scale ranges from –5 to +5, from strongly beneficial to strongly opposed, with zero representing a no effect situation.

The ratings of leverage and effect are first made in a "business as usual" environment, not in a crisis. In the case of Indonesia, the ratings can be thought of as those prevailing at the end of June 1997, before the onset of the crisis. The onset of the crisis leads to a crystallization of the positions of the CPCs with respect to various policies. Once the crisis is under way, these positions become inputs to the trade-off analyses carried out by the government in its search for a solution to the crisis. Whether explicitly stated or not, these positions help the analyst and the policymaker evaluate policy alternatives and can point toward potential trade-offs. Steadfast opposition to a policy, even in the presence of high leverage by the CPC, can be overcome by the government if the situation requires it—but at great political cost.

The relative position of the CPCs indicates the relative ease with which the government will be able to implement or enforce a given policy. If the CPCs

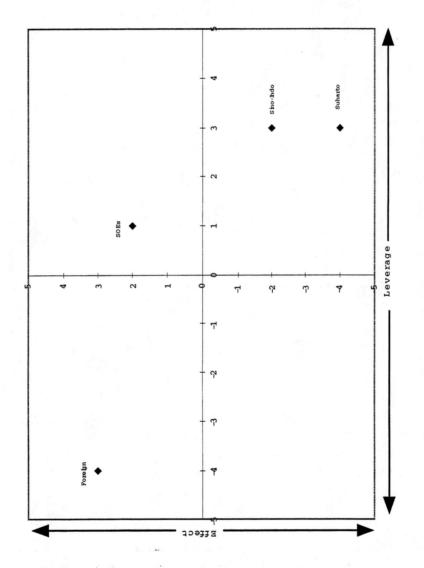

Figure 4.1—Position of CPCs Regarding Strict Banking Oversight

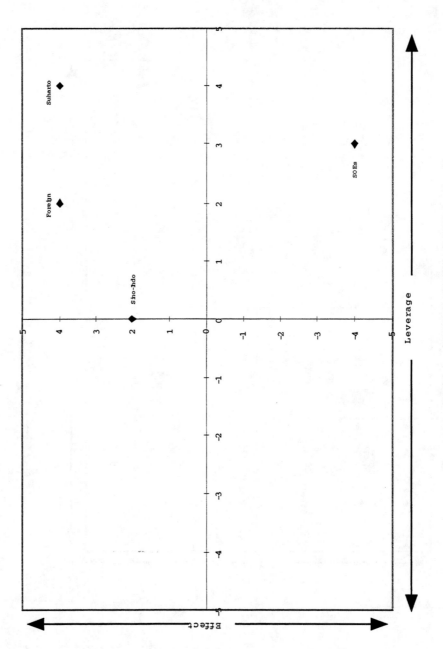

Figure 4.2—Position of CPCs Regarding SOE Privatization

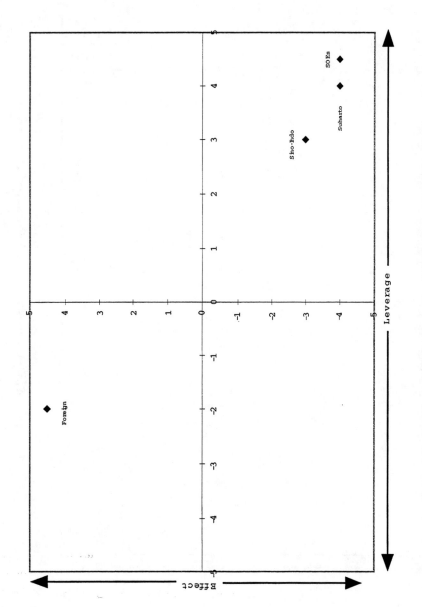

Figure 4.3—Position of CPCs Regarding Equal Treatment of Foreign Investors

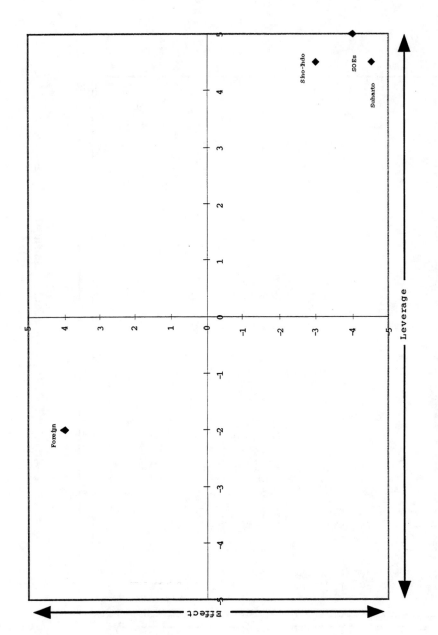

Figure 4.4—Position of CPCs Regarding Enhanced Governance

cluster in the northeast quadrant, the policy is likely to succeed, since it affects the CPCs positively, and the CPCs have leverage to see it carried out. A concentration of CPCs in the southeast quadrant, by contrast, indicates that the policy is likely to fail, since it affects CPCs negatively, and the CPCs have leverage to block or derail it. If the CPCs cluster in the southwest quadrant, they do not like the policy but probably cannot block it. Finally, a grouping of CPCs in the northwest quadrant indicates a positive disposition toward that particular policy but without much capital to implement it.

Regarding strict banking oversight, the foreign and SOE CPCs stand to gain from the policy but for different reasons. SOEs look favorably at stricter banking oversight because this affects mostly private banks and not state-owned banks. As long as the private banking sector is in transition, not to say turmoil, the Indonesian government will continue to hold its deposits in state-owned banks. (The government transferred a large amount of its deposits in state pension funds in September 1997, in an attempt to dry up liquidity.) In the longer term, however, a more efficient private banking sector will be more of a threat to state-owned banks than it is today. However, SOEs have little leverage on banking regulation.

The foreign sector also stands to benefit from a healthier banking system because foreign banks can better compete on a level playing field, and foreign firms probably appreciate doing business with efficient banks. Yet the foreign sector, too, has basically no leverage on this issue.

In contrast, the other two CPCs—Sino-Indonesian conglomerates, and Suharto and kin—stand to lose if Bank Indonesia continues to close insolvent banks and tighten oversight regulations. Suharto and kin face worse effects than the Sino-Indonesian conglomerates because they lack the "deep pockets" of the latter. Bambang's public outburst after the closing of Bank Andromeda is testimony of the real pain such a policy would bring to the Suharto kin. Both CPCs are given a ranking of 3 in terms of leverage because, despite their close connections to the presidential palace, monetary policy has historically been the purview of a small group of technical experts whom the president trusts over and above his closest friends.

Thus, CPC-based analysis reveals that this policy is likely to be implemented. CPC interests are dispersed, and none has overwhelming leverage. The government should be able to implement the policy but will have to expend considerable political capital given the negative effects on both the Sino-Indonesians and Suharto's kin.

With regard to SOE privatization, CPC interests are also dispersed. Not surprisingly, the SOEs are the staunchest opponents of privatization, and they have substantial leverage. Despite their lack of direct access to the president, SOEs and the ministries overseeing them may rely on bureaucratic inertia to stonewall privatization efforts, even if the president presses for such efforts. Thus far, the process has been proceeding at a snail's pace, despite the president's urgings and despite the appointment of a special presidential team to oversee the privatization process.[10] The IMF package shifted control over SOEs back to the Finance Ministry, away from the technical or line ministries. This constituted a major blow to the influence of SOEs, since the line ministries were their major agents of influence; officials of those ministries derived substantial perquisites and a sense of power from the control of "their" SOEs.[11] As an outcome to the IMF negotiations, we would now rank the leverage of SOEs no more than 1.5 (instead of 3 just prior to the crisis; see Figure 4.2). This alone should make the prospects for privatization bright.

Suharto's kin and the foreign sector both would be positively affected by faster privatization. Due to their connections to the president, the kin have more leverage. Buying assets from SOEs is the fastest way for both CPCs to expand their businesses. Yet both are constrained from doing so—the kin by popular resentment at wholesale purchases of government assets and the latter by economic nationalism, still alive and well in Indonesian discourse.

The Sino-Indonesians have very mixed feelings about privatization. On the one hand, from a business perspective, they are keenly interested. On the other, from a political standpoint, they are reluctant to acquire SOEs' assets for fear of a political backlash against their increased control over national production. On balance, Sino-Indonesians have available to them more diversification and growth strategies than do conglomerates controlled by Suharto's kin, so they probably would prefer a slower privatization process, which their conglomerates could more easily "digest" without popular uproar.

Hence, ramping up the privatization process is a policy that can be implemented, but a big-bang approach to privatization is not tenable politically. The process will be vulnerable the more the Indonesian economy returns to prosperity. Only

---

[10]The team was appointed by President Suharto in July 1996 and includes such political heavyweights as the Finance Minister, Mar'ie Muhammad; the Bank Indonesia governor, Soesradjad Djiwandono; and the perennial government economic advisor, Widjojo Nitisastro. See S. N. Vasuki, "Indonesia, New Team to Push Privatization," *Business Times*, Singapore, electronic version, July 13, 1997.

[11]See the discussion on channels of influence of SOEs in the case study.

if the *pribumi* (domestic non-Sino-Indonesians) acquire capital will privatization on a large scale be a viable policy option.

Regarding the third and fourth policies, equal treatment of foreign investors and transparent government procurement rules, the policy space is divided along a domestic versus foreign cleavage. In both cases, the three domestic CPCs both have strong leverage and would face negative consequences were the policies implemented. Therefore, it is likely that the policies will be carried through only under constant pressure from the international community. Even under this pressure, the Indonesian government will have to expend substantial amounts of political influence to implement the reform measures and overcome opposition from the three domestic CPCs. If both policies are—even partially— implemented, Indonesia will have come a long way toward opening itself to the outside world and truly becoming connected to the global economy.

In sum, the four policies cluster in two groups. The first two policies are characterized by an open policy space, with CPCs in different quadrants and with conflicting interests. In both cases (monetary and fiscal policy), CPC-based analysis reveals patterns of interest and can help the analyst determine whether the policy can be successfully implemented, as well as understand the potential problems and sources of opposition to the proposed policies. The last two policies confront a very similar policy space, although for different reasons. In both cases (investment deregulation and governance), the domestic-foreign dichotomy is overwhelming. The analysis underscores the prominent role the IMF and the international community would have to play if these policies were to be implemented.

5. Evaluating CPC-based Analysis

This style of analysis, using CPCs as the units to be assessed, seems most useful in judging the likelihood that given policies will be implemented. Although the international community and the U.S. government typically have not scrutinized developing economies at an industry or firm level, the reality of the "global economy" makes such an abstention costly, possibly dramatically so. Confronted with the East Asian economic turmoil, the international community has been taking a closer and closer look at the inner workings of these troubled economies.

While earlier crises tended to involve painful "structural adjustment," the latest crises have forced the IMF to address problems not captured in statistics of money supply, foreign exchange reserves, or trade balance. The IMF has had to cope with issues long raised only in World Bank reports—e.g., banking reform and better governance. As Stanley Fischer, the fund's deputy managing director observed: "What's different about the last three programs [Thailand, Indonesia, and South Korea]—and different from Mexico—is that banking- and financial-sector restructuring is absolutely at the heart of the program."[1]

This shift in emphasis by the IMF is not without risk, however. The fund has no experience as a regulator; whether it has the teeth required to make the reform program stick remains in question. Understanding the dynamics of CPCs with respect to, in this instance, banking and financial reform is a condition of success. CPC-based analysis provides useful insights into the implementation of such complex policy choices.

CPC-based analysis is hardly an exact science. It does not generate a single-point solution. Rather, the method helps the analyst characterize relationships among large influential "commercial" groups in a given emerging market. To do so, the analyst must first identify these groups, then define their respective interests and how they defend them—which channels of influence they use to promote their interests—and finally assess their leverage in seeing a particular policy implemented or canceled. The analysis suggests potential trade-offs and forces the analyst to make assumptions explicit.

---

[1]Quoted by Richard W. Stevenson and Jeff Garth, "I.M.F.'s New Look: A Deeper Role in Risky Business in Crisis Economies," *New York Times on the Web*, December 8, 1997.

Take the privatization of SOEs as an example. Conventional wisdom based on evidence from other emerging economies tends to prescribe a faster pace of privatization to generate immediate government revenues and improve overall economic efficiency. By promising to increase the pace of privatization, the Indonesian government would quickly buy itself credibility in the eyes of the IMF and foreign investors. Yet, such an approach ignores the position of CPCs: (1) the staunch opposition of SOEs to privatization, even if reduced by the transfer of oversight responsibility to the Finance Ministry; (2) the lukewarm position of the most powerful CPC in Indonesia (the Sino-Indonesian conglomerates); (3) the awkward position of Suharto's kin, despite their considerable leverage; and (4) the awkward position of foreign investors, in the face of continuing economic nationalism in Indonesian politics.

Despite over a decade of privatization efforts, the results are meager, and the process remains marginal in terms both of generating revenue and of improving overall economic efficiency. From 1988 to 1995, the Indonesian government managed 15 partial privatizations (less than 50 percent of an SOE's equity was offered publicly) and generated $4 billion—of which 40.3 percent ($1.6 billion) was in the form of foreign direct investment (FDI). This compares with Malaysia's privatization program over the same period, which generated, in 38 privatizations, $9 billion, of which 8.6 percent ($0.8 billion) came in the form of FDI.[2]

The mapping of policies (as done in Figures 4.1 through 4.4) provides a quick and intuitive glimpse at which CPC is likely to get stronger or weaker—as expressed by their position in the policy space of interest. In the case of privatization, the decision to transfer oversight responsibility to the Finance Ministry moved the SOEs from a leverage of 3 down toward 1. This judgment turned on the understanding, generated by systematic analysis of the CPC, that the main channel of influence of SOEs is the line ministries that regulate them. The mapping of the policy space also provides an intuitive understanding for how far the given policy can be pushed. In the privatization example, the fact that the Sino-Indonesian conglomerates were ambivalent might suggest seeking another policy course.

One alternative to privatizing—that is, selling—government assets might be to deregulate the industry in which SOEs compete and so level the playing field for private firms. This is the approach that Indonesia took in the banking sector. Although there the policy generated new problems stemming from lack of

---

[2]Lawrence Bouton and Mariusz A. Sumlinski, *Trends in Private Investment in Developing Countries: Statistics for 1970–95*, IFC Discussion Paper Number 31, electronic version, February 1997.

regulatory oversight, it did sharply decrease the share of the government banks
in the banking industry. Between 1983 and 1996, total bank assets controlled by
government banks decreased from 79 to 43 percent.[3] This path of deregulating
instead of privatizing has been followed in the IMF package for distribution of
some food products and cement. The CPC analysis might be used to scrutinize
various industries and map the policy space for deregulating each of them.
Comparisons among industries should offer insight into which industry ought to
be deregulated first.

The CPC-based framework of analysis is rooted in commercial interest, broadly
defined, and so must be applied with considerable art to capture strictly political
considerations. The lukewarm position of Sino-Indonesian conglomerates with
respect to privatization can only be apprehended in light of the pervasive anti-
Chinese sentiments in Indonesia. This position is mostly social and political,
even if partially grounded in economic consideration: These conglomerates do
have other avenues for growth, such as expanding into new regions.

Consider another example. The Indonesian government decided not to raise the
prices of staple goods, which are subsidized. The commodity import agency,
BULOG, retained the responsibility to stabilize supplies and prices for rice and
refined sugar. The reason probably was straightforwardly political: The
president recognized that, if prices were decontrolled, they would rise sharply
given the country's long and continuing drought. And that could well result in
riots.

Those purely political considerations would not be easily captured by the CPC-
based analysis, but, provocatively, that analysis would have suggested a similar
policy outcome for a different reason. It was very much in the interest of
Bogasari Flour Mills (part of the Salim group, the largest—Sino-Indonesian—
conglomerate in Indonesia) to maintain BULOG's regulatory control over the
import and distribution of wheat. Thus, CPC analysis would probably have
predicted no change in the regulatory environment for wheat import, milling,
and distribution.[4] In the end, the IMF package replaced the import monopoly
with a 10-percent tariff rate.

CPC-based analysis provides interesting insights into economic policymaking in
an emerging market, such as that of Indonesia. IMF interventions in Thailand,
Indonesia, and South Korea turned attention to a deeper and closer look at the

---

[3]Ross McLeod, "Country Report, Indonesia's Economic Performance, An Assessment," *Journal of
Asia Business*, Vol. 12, No. 4, 1996, pp. 77–78.

[4]For a description of the wheat trade and the vested interest of Bogasari, see Adam Schwarz, *A
Nation in Waiting*, United States: Westview Press, 1994, pp. 110-111.

economy of these countries, with particular emphasis on the banking and financial sectors. However, the analytical instruments traditionally used by the IMF and the international community at large are not adequate for understanding the dynamics of economic change at the industry level in these countries. CPC analysis provides a more micro view of the economy and provides insights into which policies are most likely to be successfully implemented. Yet it maintains a high-enough level of aggregation not to require the in-depth analysis of every industry or particular actor that may be affected by a proposed reform measure. It makes trade-off analyses explicit and helps both analysts and the policymakers think through the political cost associated with a policy option, and so helps them make better decisions.

6. Looking Across the Cases

In each of our four cases, we used a matrix to display judgments. With power centers on one axis and the "policy space" on the other, the matrix turned out to be useful not only as a way of assembling insights about particular emerging markets but also of making comparisons across them. In each cell is indicated (1) where the power center stands on a particular issue; (2) what channels it has used to try to influence policy; (3) how effective it has been; and, perhaps, (4) indications of whether its influence is waxing or waning. Indicating which policies are most important to a particular center, by marking them in bold, provides a sense of priority.

To look across the cases, the power centers can usefully be grouped by relative effectiveness, high, medium, or low (see Tables 6.1 through 6.3). (This judgment is relative; recall that all the centers were selected because their influence was notable.) At the same time, their primary channel of influence can be noted, along with whether their clout is increasing or diminishing. That might suggest that primary targets for intelligence would be those centers whose influence is high, whose clout is increasing, and whose primary channel of influence is not very transparent.

This ranking suggests a number of observations:

- The high-effectiveness grouping includes both "old" and "new" power centers, both SOEs and exporters. The same is true for the low-effectiveness grouping. The dynamic of influence does, however, mostly point in the expected direction: Old centers, such as SOEs or armies, are declining in influence, while newer ones, such as exporters or foreign investors, are increasing. The exceptions reflect particular circumstances—for instance, the military's role in Turkey.

- The countries are, as a group, still very much in transition, both economically and politically. And they vary considerably. All retain quite centralized, administratively guided state apparatuses; for instance, in none, with the partial exception of Mexico, are legislatures of much importance, and competitive party systems are not yet sufficiently developed to make electoral channels of influence very visible.

Table 6.1

**Centers of High Effectiveness, with Channel of Impact
and Dynamic of Influence**

Country	Center	Channel	Dynamic of Influence
Mexico	Manufactured and mining exporters	Electoral/ functional	Increasing
Turkey	Military	Formal/ functional	Increasing
China	Village and townships & enterprises	Formal/ functional	Increasing
	State-owned enterprises	Functional	Decreasing
Indonesia	Suharto and kin	Functional/ perhaps corruptive	Increasing
	Foreign investment	Forced/ formal	Increasing
	Sino-Indonesian	Formal/ functional/ corruptive?	Increasing

Table 6.2

**Centers of Medium Effectiveness, with Channel of Impact
and Dynamic of Influence**

Country	Center	Channel	Dynamic of Influence
Mexico	Landowners of the north	Formal/ functional	Stagnant
Turkey	Islamists, MUSIAD	Formal and possibly corruptive	Decreasing- short run
	Secular holding companies, and USIAD	Formal/ functional	Increasing
	Unions	Forced/ formal	Decreasing
China	"Princelings" enterprises	Functional/ perhaps corruptive	Decreasing
	PLA-related industry	Formal/ functional	Decreasing
Indonesia	State-owned enterprises	Functional/ formal	Stable to receding

Table 6.3

**Centers of Low Effectiveness, with Channel of Impact and
Dynamic of Influence**

Country	Center	Channel	Dynamic of Influence
Mexico	Indians and the EZLN	Forced	Decreasing
China	Foreign-owned enterprises	Formal	Increasing

- Mexico is the furthest along on the political path, though not the economic; China is the least, with Indonesia and Turkey somewhere in between. China and its power centers were hard to characterize, because its decentralization, perhaps more *de facto* than *de jure*, is striking in economic terms, but the country is far from politically plural, at least by western standards.

- Indeed, the analysis raises intriguing questions about China's direction. Put starkly, will China move toward a *chaebol*-like system or a truly open economy? It is worth noting, though, that there is no necessary connection between a high degree of agglomeration in industrial organization internally and closedness to foreigners externally. Japan's *keiretsu* did combine the two, though there was fierce competition at home. Given its geography and heterogeneity relative to Japan, China is unlikely to mimic Japan's MITI. At worst, it could wind up with a degraded Japanese system, with large conglomerates that were not very competitive internally but remained closed to outsiders.

- Identifying channels of influence was the trickiest part of the project. We expected there would be systematic change in channels of influence across countries. Logically, as economies emerge and political systems develop, there should be movement away from opaque, informal, especially "corruptive," forms of influence toward more regular, institutional, and transparent ones. The distinction might be thought of between *particularist* forms of influence highly dependent on personal connections and more *institutionalized* forms of systematic lobbying aimed a broader influence over policy.

The ranking does hint at such a pattern, though caution is in order in interpreting that result, for several reasons. One is that the sample size is small and the evidence skimpy. Another is that particular circumstances or personalities matter a lot, especially in the short run. And policy and business cultures reflect more than stage of development; they also reflect national cultures. At any given point in their political and economic transitions, China and Mexico will be very different simply because their traditions and cultures are so different.

- Finally, for intelligence, the logical focus of concentration is those power centers that are both *opaque* and *important*. That would suggest attention to the Turkish military and, secondarily, to the Islamist and MUSIAD; to China's village and township enterprises and, still, to SOEs; and to Suharto and his circle and to the Sino-Indonesians. Here, the implications of the analysis run more to *what* intelligence should look for than *how* it should look for it. We have identified emerging power centers as objects of analysis, but those might have been identified in some other way. But this analysis has suggested hypotheses, along with indicators to watch. For instance, the insight that the power, at least economic, of the Chinese princelings should decline as the economy matures is an intriguing one. It also implies indicators to watch.

Appendix

A. Evidence from the Cases: Mexico

Mexico's Economic Strategy and the Power Centers

Given Mexico's economic strategy, three newer power centers were salient, while three others remained important[1]:

- Indians and anti-government guerrillas

- Landowners of the north

- Exporters of manufactured and mining-related products

- PRI

- Labor unions (Consejo de Trabajadores de México)

- The army.

The influence of power centers in Mexico is framed by that country's economic transformation over the last generation and, in particular, by the aftermath of that transformation's crisis in 1994–1995. Mexico's development strategy rests on two pillars: (1) opening the economy to market forces while reducing the role of the state and (2) inserting Mexico into the international economy through liberalizing its international trade and promoting competitiveness in the private sector. Two cleavages run consistently through the discussion of specific power centers. First, while Mexico's opening aims to promote competitiveness both externally and internally, policies designed to promote openness, and especially to spur exports, often run directly against the stakes of those trying to protect shares of the domestic market, often with some protection. Second, while industry and services are the dynamic sectors of the economy, Mexico's agriculture, obsolete though it is, still employs over a fifth of the labor force and thus bears heavily on domestic stability.

Given that strategy, the policy space of interest to the centers includes:

---

[1]Mexico's fifty-odd commercial banks might be considered a power center but have not been here. A majority of those banks are associated with holdings within the industrial sector. Moreover, the newly privatized commercial banks have been beset with problems almost from the outset. Between 1994 and 1995, the ratio of bad debts to the banking system's total portfolio had risen from 8.3 percent to 17.2 percent, and the rescue package is costing the government approximately 24 billion USD.

1. Monetary, fiscal, and exchange-rate policy, where the policy outcome has been tight policies on the first two and a managed float in exchange rates.

2. Regulation (price, interest rates, and wages), where deregulation has been the order of the day, though with stickiness in labor markets.

3. International trade, where the capstone is the North American Free Trade Agreement (NAFTA), and the policy is opening borders to foreign competition and promoting exports.

4. International capital. Mexico's domestic savings fall far short of the level of investment needed to modernize the economy, so the country is opening to foreign investment, both portfolio and direct.

5. Privatization, where President Ernesto Zedillo has continued the policies of his predecessor, most notably in communications, transport, and part of the oil sector.

6. Land reform

7. Environmental regulation

8. Reform of the political system.

Table A.1 summarizes the centers, their actions with respect to the policy space, and the success of those actions. The shaded cells indicate policies of special priority to the particular center.

Assessing the Mexican Case

What is first striking about the Mexican power centers is the difference in the breadth of their interests. Of the three main centers, the one we defined most broadly, manufacture and mining exporters, has interests across the range of policy space. At the other extreme, the northern landowners' stakes are quite specific—for corn producers, it is corn prices and subsidies for credit and other inputs. For other crop producers, the stake extends to policy with regard to agricultural imports or to land reform. The third center, the Indians and guerrillas, also has broad interests, if vaguer ones. Because its interests are more political than economic in character, they are stated at a higher level of generality.

As the table suggests, the observed changes in Mexican policy are, broadly, those favored by the group of exporters of manufactured and mining products. The only exception is the reform of the political system, where the center strongly favors the status quo—after all, it developed under the set of current laws and property rights. Moreover, the center has established solid links at different

Table A.1
Mexico's CPCs and the Policy Space

Policy	Element	Indians and the EZLN	Land Owners of the North Region	Exporters	PRI	Unions (CTM)	Army
Monetary	Aim	Favor an expansive policy	Favor low interest rates and thus a relaxation of monetary policy	Favor a conservative monetary policy	Favors a restrictive monetary policy consistent with price stability	Leaders support restrictive monetary policy and low inflation targets	Supports government's restrictive monetary policy
	Channel	Executive power–forced	Not established for this policy	Executive power–electoral/functional	Executive power–functional	Executive power–formal	
	Effectiveness	Very low	NA	High	High	Medium	
	Dynamic	Negotiations have slowed down	No change	No change	The PRI has moved to more conservative policy compared to the 70's	Change with respect to policies supported during the 70's	
Fiscal	Aim	Demand increases in subsidies and social expenditure	Demand increases in subsidies for the sector	Demand a reduction in public expenditures	Reluctant to cut public expenditures given political costs	Leaders support a reduction in the public deficit	Demands an increase in the defense budget
	Channel	Executive power–forced	Congress –formal	Executive power–electoral/ functional; congress–electoral	Congress–functional; executive power–functional	Executive power–formal	Executive power–formal
	Effectiveness	Low	Low	High	Medium	Medium	High
	Dynamic	Negotiations have slowed down	No change	No change	PRI's vision of the use of fiscal policy has become more conservative	Change with respect to the 70's where unions supported an expansive fiscal policy	Effectiveness has increased as a consequence of the guerrilla and drug traffic

Table A.1—Continued

Policy	Element	Indians and the EZLN	Land Owners of the North Region	Exporters	PRI	Unions (CTM)	Army
Real Exchange Rate	Aim	Oppose devaluation of the exchange rate	Favor a real depreciation of the exchange rate that increases the cost of the imports of cereal	Demand a floating exchange rate	Favors intervention policies that stabilize the exchange rate given the political cost of devaluations	Leaders support exchange rate liberalization executive powerformal	Supports government managed flotation
	Channel	Executive power–forced	Not established for this policy	Executive power–electoral/functional	Executive power–functional	Executive power–formal	
	Effectiveness	Very low	NA	Medium	Medium	Medium	
	Dynamic	Negotiations have slowed down	No change	Effectiveness increased after the crisis of 1994	PRI has moved to support a more market based management of the exchange rate compared to the 70's	Change with respect to the policy supported during the 70's	
International trade	Aim	Oppose liberalization	Oppose the liberalization of imports of cereals	Demand liberalization	Favors liberalization	Cautious about liberalization given the short run effects on employment	Supports government outward oriented strategy
	Channel	Executive power–forced	Congress–formal	Executive power–electoral/functional; congress–electoral	Executive power–functional; congress–functional	Congress–formal/forced	
	Effectiveness	Very low	Low	High	High	Medium	
	Dynamic	Negotiations have slowed down	No change	Effectiveness has increased	PRI has moved to support an outward oriented strategy instead of the old import substitution strategy	Have become more supportive of outward oriented policies	

Table A.1—Continued

Policy	Element	Indians and the EZLN	Land Owners of the North Region	Exporters	PRI	Unions (CTM)	Army
Foreign capitals	Aim	Oppose entrance of foreign capitals	Indifferent	Demand deregulation of foreign investment	Favors deregulation but considers important to maintain restrictions in strategic areas	Cautious about foreign investment	Supports government deregulatory policy
	Channel	Executive power—forced	NA	Executive power—electoral/functional; congress—electoral	Executive power—functional; congress—functional	Congress—formal/forced	
	Effectiveness	Very low	NA	High	High	Medium	
	Dynamic	Negotiations have slowed down	No change	No change	PRI has become more open regarding foreign investment	Have become more supportive of outward oriented policies	
External Debt	Aim	Oppose payment	Indifferent	Encourage negotiation of future payments	Encourages negotiation of future payments	Encourage negotiation of reductions in debt	Supports government negotiations with international organization and other governments
	Channel	Executive power—forced	NA	Executive power—formal	Executive power—functional	Executive power—formal/forced	
	Effectiveness	Very low	NA	Medium	Medium	Low	
	Dynamic	Negotiations have slowed down	No change	No change	No change	No change	

Table A.1—Continued

Policy	Element	Indians and the EZLN	Land Owners of the North Region	Exporters	PRI	Unions (CTM)	Army
Privatization	Aim	Oppose privatization	Indifferent	Demand dynamism in the privatization process	Supports privatizations but is cautious with some areas such as oil	Cautious about privatization, consider that workers should have access to the capital	Favors privatization of those companies not belonging to the armed forces
	Channel	Executive power–forced	NA	Congress–electoral/functional	Congress–functional	Executive power–formal/forced; congress–formal/forced	Executive power–formal
	Effectiveness	Very low	NA	High	Medium		High
	Dynamic	Negotiations have slowed down	No change	Effectiveness has increased	Has changed its vision of the role of the public sector in the economy compared to the 70's	Change with respect to the anti private sector policies favored during the 70's	No change
Regulatory policies	Aim	Favor regulation	Increase or eliminate price ceilings	Demand market deregulation	Cautious about deregulation specially of the labor market given the political costs	Cautious about deregulation, specifically basic consumption products and the labor market	Supports deregulation
	Channel	Executive power–forced	Executive power–(Secofi) formal; congress–formal/electoral	Congress–electoral/functional	Congress–electoral	Congress–formal/forced	
	Effectiveness	Very low	Medium	Medium	Medium	Medium	
	Dynamic	Negotiations have slowed down	Before 1993 producers enjoyed price floors, today they face price ceilings	Effectiveness has increased	Has converged to a more market oriented vision of the economy compared to 70's	No change	

Table A.1—Continued

Policy	Element	Indians and the EZLN	Land Owners of the North Region	Exporters	PRI	Unions (CTM)	Army
Land Reform	Aim	Demand redistribution of land	Oppose land reform, demand protection of private property	Unclear	Would support land reform but has not introduced the subject in the congress agenda	Would support land reform	Supports status quo
	Channel	Executive power–forced	Executive power–formal	NA	Not defined for this policy		
	Effectiveness	Very low	High	NA		NA	
	Dynamic	Negotiations have slowed down	No change	No change		NA	
Reform of the Political System	Aim	Demand elimination of the PRI government	Unclear	Oppose the reform of the political system	"Old guard" of the PRI opposes structural reforms	Unclear: leaders would lose control under the reform	Opposes reform given strong ties with the current government
	Channel	Executive power–forced	NA	Executive power–electoral; congress–electoral	Executive power–functional; congress–functional	Congress –formal	Executive power–formal
	Effectiveness	Medium	NA	Low /medium	Medium	Unclear	Medium
	Dynamic	Negotiations have slowed down	No change	Effectiveness has decreased	Effectiveness has declined in part given the pressure generated by the EZLN	Unclear	No change

Table A.1—Continued

Policy	Element	Indians and the EZLN	Land Owners of the North Region	Exporters	PRI	Unions (CTM)	Army
Environmental Regulations	Aim	Demand redistribution of land	Favor regulations	Oppose strong regulations	It is not interested in strong regulations	Would support environmental regulations	Supports government policies
	Channel	Executive power—forced	Not established for this policy	Congress—electoral	Congress—functional	Not defined for this policy	
	Effectiveness	Very low	NA	High	High	NA	
	Dynamic	Negotiations have slowed down	No change	Effectiveness is likely to go down in the future given the pressure of environmentalists	No change	NA	

levels of the administration. It has used mainly functional linkages to influence public policy, with its members appointed to public portfolios. Indeed, it has been a key player in implementing Mexico's current development strategy. Its role is likely to continue to strengthen.

The Indians and guerrillas have generally been the losers in policy outcomes. The only exception is partial: While mainstream groups were the main campaigners for the reforms of the political system initiated by Zedillo, those reforms were also partly a response to the pressures generated by the EZLN (Ejército Zapatista de Liberación Nacional) and kindred social groups reacting to 70 years of PRI government. The changes so far have been modest but amount to the first step in a process of democratizing the Mexican system. The EZLN has forced the executive power to negotiate (forced linkage), but as Table A.1 shows, the EZLN has been ineffective.

Nevertheless, the Indians and the guerrillas will retain a role as social filters of government policies. Even if they could be neutralized militarily, they represent an important constraint for governmental policy—for instance, on public expenditure, the environment, and foreign investment. It is important to remember that their actions contributed to the climate of uncertainty that induced foreign capital to flee Mexico in 1994. Furthermore, these types of movements are proliferating, and they indirectly put pressure on a more socially oriented development strategy.

Corn producers—and other crop producers whose products are sold primarily on the domestic market—appear as a conservative force favoring the status quo in such areas as international trade and economic liberalization. This center has tried to influence policy mainly through formal linkages, such as the National Confederation of Rural Property Owners (CNPR). In Table A.1, we observe that the effectiveness has been low. However, this center remains an important employer, and thus its collapse would be costly from a social and political perspective. The government is aware of this, and so this center will retain influence over NAFTA-related policies.

The objectives of the PRI might be abstracted to maximizing both the votes it receives in different elections and the length of time it can remain in power. Given this objective, the interests of the PRI with regard to different parts of the policy space should adapt to changes in the balance of political forces. When reactionary and progressive forces are in rough balance, the PRI should tend to preserve the status quo. For most of the policies under analysis, the interests of the PRI and of the government moved in the same direction, but the PRI is more cautious. With regard to economic policy, the PRI's interests diverge from those of the government: To the extent that economic reforms appear to threaten social peace, the PRI will oppose them.

Because of the political reforms and because new generations are starting to take over important positions—symbolized recently by the death of labor boss Fidel Velasquez—important changes will be introduced inside the party. The PRI will still be an important political force, but it will lose its monopoly in the political "market" because of competition from the ideas and projects of other groups.

Unions—or at least their leaders—have assented to the government's economic plan. However, were unions unconstrained by the process of co-option practiced by the government, their interests might move in the other direction. Union strength, for instance, is concentrated in domestic firms and public enterprises that are more threatened than advantaged by restructuring and the growth of exports.

Recent political reforms have weakened the iron triangle composed of the CTM (Confederación de Trabajadores de México), the PRI, and the government. So, two possible future scenarios can be envisaged. In the first, and less likely, Mexican workers will reorganize and redefine common interests outside the set of constraints that were imposed by the CTM and the PRI. A new union of workers independent of government will appear and become an important social force, hence an important lever for public policy.

In the second and more likely scenario, small groups that now are permitted to organize will proliferate but in fact have no political power. "Worker" will have little meaning as a unifying concept. There will be different dynamics within different sectors of the economy, and even different regions, and these will produce different "contracts" between firms and the labor force—for instance, the export sector as opposed to corn production.

The interests of the army run in parallel with government policy along most of the dimensions of the policy space. The exception is fiscal policy, where the army prefers a reduction in fiscal constraints, given that its budget is affected. More important, though, the army is being thrust more and more into governance despite its inclinations. It is becoming more and more of a *political* power, though its preferences on the dimension of this analysis remain unclear or are yet to be shaped.

In the Mexican case, the Indians and guerrillas acquire economic power, mostly indirectly, because they have political power. The center has that power because they can mobilize and because they receive support from other elements of the Mexican population. For the exporters, the reverse is very nearly true: They have political power because they have economic clout. Thinking about the source of the exporters' power, though, takes analysis to the next dimension, its links to government policy, for it is both the creature and the supporter of government policy. It supports, and is in turn supported by, government policy.

B. Evidence from the Cases: Turkey

Turkey's Economic Policy and the Power Centers

Turkey's power centers are

- the Turkish military
- leading secular businesses (TUSIAD) and others
- Islamic business interests (MUSIAD) and the Refah Party
- trade unions
- the illegal sector.[1]

Three trends in the political economy of Turkey shape the workings of the power centers and their effects:

- The Ataturk legacy of secularism, westernization, and statism has come under increasing strain, with mixed effects. On one hand is the rise of political Islam. On the other are diverse pressures on the legacy of state enterprise that is difficult to dismantle.

- The government is more and more paralyzed, and the traditional political class is dissolving, producing a kind of "darker version" of the Italian model.

- CPCs are, however, becoming more institutionalized and more diverse.

The visible source of Turkey's economic instability has been large public sector deficits—about a tenth of GDP in 1996—whose root cause is the large and inefficient state economic enterprises (SEEs). Between a third and a half of the deficit is attributable to recent decisions to speed retirement for state workers, which, despite Turkey's relatively young population, leaves each pensioner supported by only two contributors. Moreover, Turkey's tax collection is spotty.

---

[1]The illegal sector might have been broken out as a center for most of the countries under analysis. Illegal activity, once under way, probably benefits from economic openness: Mushrooming trade along the U.S.-Mexican border makes drug smuggling easier. That said, the root of illegal economic activity often is a political structure that restricts, regulates, or proscribes certain transactions, such as those involving drugs or weapons. What seemed to distinguish Turkey from the others was the clarity of the illegal sector's stakes in the policy space. By contrast, in Mexico, the interests of the illegal activity, heavily drug-related, did not reach very clearly into the economic policy space under consideration.

The lurking concern is worsening income distribution, both between the haves and the have nots countrywide and between the poorer east and southeast Anatolia and the west—all the more a concern given the stagnation of agriculture.

On the positive side, the Turkish private sector is dynamic, though much of it is "unregistered" or "informal"—perhaps as many as half the workers are in that sector. International trade has increased substantially, both absolutely and as a proportion of GNP, since the beginning of the Ozal liberalization program of the 1980s. Total merchandise trade has jumped from $4.7 billion in 1979 (16 percent of GNP) to $45.4 billion in 1993 (25 percent of GNP). Foreign direct investment (FDI) has been and continues to be relatively small, given both the size and growth of the domestic economy, and the last year of political instability. FDI in recent years peaked in 1993, amounting to a modest $797 million gross, or about 0.4 percent of GNP. Whether Turkey will remain perpetually on the verge of "take off" will depend on what policies result from the constellation of political forces in which the power centers act.

The policy space of concern to those centers is as follows:

1. Privatization and structural reform, where the current driver is more the need for revenue than a strong commitment to basic change.

2. Defense-industrial policy, where deference to the military, as well as the security outlook on Turkey's borders, has produced a large defense plan.

3. Relations with the European Union (EU) and the customs union, the most charged issue in Turkey, where the Turkish drive for full membership is strong, especially among the western-oriented elites, but the prospects are poorer and poorer.

4. Energy policy, where a looming crisis is perceived as a major constraint on growth.

5. Trade and investment among adjacent regions, where key issues are subsidies to Turkish Cyprus, trade ties to the Caucasus and central Asia, and economic ties to Israel.

6. The southeast, where poverty collides with the Kurdish insurgency to give the government a strong incentive to promote development and thus to try to stem separatism.

Table B.1 summarizes the Turkish power centers, their actions, effect and priority interests.

Table B.1

Turkish CPCs and the Policy Space

	Economic Reform & Privatization	EU/Customs Union	Defense Procurement	Southeastern Anatolia	New Energy Ties	Regional Trade	Banking & Finance Reform
Military	Ambivalent	Favor	Oppose civil control	Favor central investment	Geopolitical interest	Favor, but Euro-centric	Status Quo
Islamists (RP, MUSIAD, Hak-IS)	Favor for revenue, patronage	Oppose but tolerate	Favor civil control	Strong ties, favor investment	Favor	Seek realignment to East, South	Pragmatic
Secular Holding Companies (TUSIAD)	Favor	Favor (with exceptions)	Consider reform, but stake in status quo	Explore political change	Favor	Active, but Euro-centric	Status quo (self-financing)
Unions	Strongly oppose	Ambivalent					
Illegal Sector	Against	Against		Benefit from "war economy"		"Suitcase" stake	Favor (lax) status quo

NOTE: Areas of high interest and/or engagement are shaded.

Assessing the Turkey Case

Summing up the Turkish business culture, a dynamic private sector has emerged as a counterweight to the large state sector and statist economic outlook inherited from Ataturk, but many limitations remain. The large holding companies that are a leading feature of the Turkish economic landscape are not at the cutting edge of quality management and business analysis and remain tied to traditional patterns of family ownership and control. Few companies, for instance, have sought to attract equity financing from foreign investors. Concerns over loss of family control and the associated lack of flexibility in the recruitment of management have emerged as leading impediments to FDI and joint ventures with Turkish enterprises. Major private-sector enterprises continue to contend with a high degree of policy uncertainty and economic vulnerability in their dealings with the state.

The Turkish state, including the military, retains enormous weight in the Turkish economy, but its "competence" and ability to control economic activity is declining. A recent survey indicates that, of the 500 largest industrial corporations in 1995, 55 were public companies, accounting for 33 percent of total sales. In 1994, 71 state-owned companies accounted for 40 percent of the top 500's sales. Progress in the current privatization drive will curtail the economic influence of the state even further. This tendency is also manifesting itself in less promising ways, not least the rise of a large and assertive illegal sector with ties to the political class and state bureaucracies.

Key power centers are important stakeholders in the struggle between Turkey's "statists" and those seeking economic reform. The military and the public-sector unions are clearly in the former camp, with a strong preference for existing patterns of state ownership and control. Elsewhere, this debate cuts across power center lines. In Islamist circles, Refah is reluctant to dismantle state enterprises (except for purposes of revenue) or to end traditional subsidies, but many of its private-sector supporters display a more reformist outlook. Some large secular enterprises and organizations (e.g., TUSIAD) have been on the cutting edge of advocacy for structural change and a more international outlook, while others fear the loss of subsidies and preferential relationships.

The Islamist Refah Party appears to be building a substantial business constituency, largely drawn from small and medium enterprises (including the "Anatolian Lions"). Some large, traditionally secular holding companies are also developing a more tolerant approach to Refah, although most leading holding companies remain strongly opposed to the Islamists and their populist economic agenda. To the extent that Refah—or something like it—remains a force on the

Turkish scene, it is likely to extend its already considerable efforts to promote the interests of sympathetic businesses (and religious sects with ties to private enterprises). This would represent a significant change in traditional patterns of state patronage, to the disadvantage of the large secular holding companies. Recent political turmoil in Turkey—which led to the resignation of the Refah prime minister Necmettin Erbakan—has weakened the Islamist center's influence, at least in the short run. That said, the military's concern was also demonstrated by its recent attempts to rein in holding companies with Islamist ties.

With the striking exception of the activities of TUSIAD and the Foreign Economics Relations Board (DEIK), which are increasingly aimed at influencing the informed public and decisionmakers on national-level policy issues, Turkish power centers remain attached to traditional, "preferential" approaches in their interaction with the government. Direct, personal access to decisionmakers is still the preferred, indeed essential, mode of influence.

Figure B.1 is a type of influence diagram, portraying graphically which centers counter each other and which are mutually reinforcing.

This diagram summarizes the interrelationships between the five Turkish CPCs. Linkages between the centers are shown by arrows, and the direction of the arrow illustrates the main thrust of the relationship. A plus or minus sign placed next to the center's arrow implies whether the CPCs have a cooperative and beneficial or adversarial and harmful connection. For instance, an increase in the power of the military is likely to be good for the secular holding companies, and

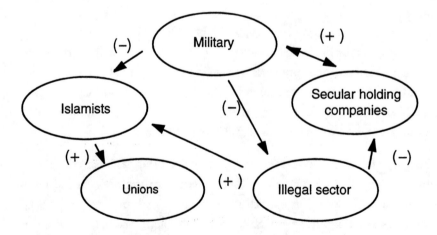

Figure B.1—Interrelationships Among Turkish CPCs—A First Attempt

vice versa, so the positive arrow goes in both directions. By contrast, the Islamists may not have much effect on the illegal sector, but growth of illegal activity is likely to increase the influence of those Islamists who fulminate for "clean hands" in Turkish business and governance—thus, the positive arrow runs one way from the illegal sector to the Islamists.

From the perspective of what is new and worth following in Turkey's emerging politics, two items stand out: First is the extent and character of Refah's emerging support among the "Anatolian Lions" and others and the meaning of this rapidly developing relationship for Turkish policy, especially regional investment and the privatization agenda. Private sector influences could well have a moderating effect on Refah's populist and nationalist economic instincts.

Second, the policy analyses and advocacy of TUSIAD and its private-sector patrons are worth watching. Many Turkish and foreign observers believe that a viable centrist political alternative to Refah is most likely to emerge from the reform-minded private sector. MUSIAD's thinking on economic and commercial questions may be a valuable guide to what we can expect from this quarter. Similarly, evidence of panic from within this power center would be a significant indicator of coming instability in Turkish economy and society.

Developments in Turkey's illegal sector and revelations about the role of the state (including the military) in drug-trafficking, money laundering, and narco-terrorism could have a substantial effect on the character of bilateral relations as a whole, not just on investment decisions made by American or other foreign companies. A clearer understanding of these linkages is necessary.

Finally, the stark terms of the EU's most recent discourse about Turkish membership could have a marked effect on Turkey's own debate about Europe. Important power centers, including the military and leading private enterprises, have for the most part put aside their particular concerns about the commercial and adjustment costs of closer integration, because the political stakes seemed so high and the potential consequences for the country's future orientation so critical. If the objective of membership is clearly unattainable, these narrower objections (e.g., on subsidies and harmonization) may prove decisive and throw new weight behind the anti-Europe lobby. This would, in turn, place greater pressure on bilateral relations with the U.S. across the board.

C. Evidence from the Cases: China

China's Power Centers

In general, major centers in China can be grouped into two categories—the traditional power centers which existed before the reform began, and the newly emerged centers, which were born through the process of economic reform. The traditional power centers include the following:

- PLA-related industries and enterprises (including defense industries and PLA conglomerates)

- Princelings' (*Taizidang*) enterprises

- SOEs.

The new power centers include the following:

- Village and township enterprises (VTEs)

- Individual and private enterprises

- Foreign investment enterprises

- PLA-linked enterprises. These accounted for 6.4 percent of total Chinese exports in 1995. Also called defense industry enterprises (DIEs), they have had some success in moving into civilian products, but they also confront the problems of SOEs more generally: weak management, poor quality and poor marketing. Moreover, perhaps 60 percent of the DIEs are located in the so-called "Third Front," remote mountainous areas of the interior. Perhaps only a third, or even fewer, operate in the black.

- "Princelings" enterprises. This special group of people has easy access to political power, the family members of political leaders, often their sons or daughters, the so-called "*taizidang*," or "princeling party." Since the economic reform in 1978, the Chinese Communist Party has allowed its retired officials and children of political leaders to engage in business. After nearly 18 years, these people have formed a special class and have built up their economic kingdoms all over the nation. The princelings are better educated, more managerial, and, perhaps, less ideological than their parents.

- SOEs. These have been stable in terms of employment, 44 million in 1995, or 25 percent of the urban workforce. However, they have been growing much more slowly than the economy as a whole; they accounted for 65 percent of industrial output in 1985 but only about a third by 1995. They are also declining rapidly in terms of exports, from about 85 percent of the total in 1986 to less than a third by 1993.

  The SOEs are in decline for a variety of reasons. Some are obvious, like inefficiency and lack of incentive. But they also support a large share of Chinese social-welfare expenditures in housing, education, and the like. For all their decline, they still benefit from preferential credit and other subsidies and still comprise seven-tenths of China's industrial assets, including the "commanding heights" of steel, oil, and telecommunications.

- VTEs. These, which grew out of earlier people's communes, are concentrated in food and consumer goods and services. Appearing from nowhere, in Deng Xiaoping's reported words, they now account for 20 percent of China's employment, 28 percent in rural areas; account for 40 percent of China's exports; and are growing rapidly.

  That said, they face challenges. Many are located in remote areas where infrastructure is lacking. Their managers are often ill-trained and inexperienced, and they no longer benefit from the government preferences that they enjoyed in earlier years. They will face increasing competition not only from the private sector but from newly freed SOEs.

- Private-sector enterprises. The Chinese private sector is composed of *getihu*, or individual enterprises, and *siyinqiye*, or private enterprises. Firms with fewer than eight employees are considered individual enterprises. Private enterprises boomed in 1992-1993 after a famous state intervention, Deng's southern tour, particularly in the eastern coastal provinces where the economy itself was booming. Individual enterprises are mostly engaged in local services, while the private enterprises are larger, often much larger, and engage in trade, manufacturing, and even high technology. The productivity of the individual enterprises is only half that of VTEs and a quarter that of SOEs, but the private enterprises are much more productive, about twice as productive per worker as VTEs.

The policy space of interest to the centers comprises:

Monetary Policy

Traditional monetary policy in western countries consists of reserve requirements, interest rate policy, and open market operations. However, in China, where the banking system is controlled by the state and where there is a lack of mature bond market and money market, monetary policy is often equivalent to credit allocation. In fact, the major role of the state banks is to receive deposits from the public and make loans to SOEs. The exercise and effectiveness of monetary policy are dramatically limited by the rudimentary state of China's banking system—for instance, the obscure connections between the finance ministry and the various state banks, both national and provincial.

After 1992, the Chinese economy entered a period of high growth with double-digit inflation. The retail price index grew by 22 percent and 15 percent in 1994 and 1995, respectively. However, the economy slowed down in 1996 and achieved a soft landing, with the inflation rate down to single digits.

Fiscal Policy

In China, government spending, especially investment spending, is the major tool of its fiscal policy. A significant part of government investment goes to the SOEs—in 1993 they absorbed 61 percent of total investment in fixed assets. Another part of government spending that goes to SOEs is the subsidies to those enterprises that run deficits. In 1995, subsidies *to* SOEs accounted for 43 percent of income tax revenue *from* SOEs. In recent years, this type of subsidy has been declining both in absolute level and as a share of GDP, reflecting government policy changes toward SOEs.

An important issue in tax policy is the emergence of fiscal federalism—the decline of the central government's share in tax revenue. From 1978 to 1994, the share of the central government in budgetary revenue declined from 59 to 41 percent. However, its expenditure fell only from 46 percent to 41 percent. As a result, the central government's fiscal deficit enlarged, generating upward pressure on price levels. The deficit also undermined the central government's ability to invest in badly needed areas, such as energy, transportation and infrastructure.

While much of the decline in central revenue resulted from the declining fortunes of the SOEs, administrative decentralization also played a role. Before 1995, revenues were divided among central, provincial, and local governments through a complex contractual system, under which revenues were raised by local tax authorities and then shared with the central government through a preset contract. This created an incentive for local governments to exempt their enterprises, especially VTEs, at the expense of the center. The rapid expansion of VTEs, which are under the control of local authorities, contributed to the growth of the "off-budget" revenue of local governments and thus provided a strong incentive for local governments to promote and defend the interests of "their" VTEs.

The response to these problems was a comprehensive tax reform in 1994, which separated central taxes from local taxes and reorganized the tax collecting services into national tax services and local tax services. In this way, the central government endeavored to collect more revenue from provincial and local governments, especially the rich provinces in the east coastal regions, such as Guangdong. Not surprisingly, perhaps, the policy was initiated as early as 1991 but was not implemented until the middle of 1994, precisely because of the resistance from Guangdong and other eastern coastal provinces.

Trade Policy

The major trade policy issue is accession to the World Trade Organization (WTO), and the focus of the discussion is on China's trade barriers, both tariff barriers and non-tariff barriers (NTBs), such as import licenses and subsidies. In recent years, China has reduced the former, but the latter are still pervasive, and China still has considerably more formal trade barriers than any other major economy. Under the conditions set by the United States and other western countries, China would have to open its market further, taking steps that would bear heavily on domestic industries and enterprises.

China's legal system poses another obstacle to WTO membership. In China, trade regulations and policies are set by the central government, but their implementation in different provinces is inconsistent, and sometimes the laws are simply not enforced. This has been a particularly serious problem for the protection of intellectual property rights (IPR). The United States has criticized China for not enforcing the bilateral agreement on IPR protection. In defense, China cites the lack of central government control over provincial governments— a claim hardly unheard of in the United States—as well as the obstacles that arise because some of the operations are under the control of the military.

Other barriers to China's joining the WTO include the so-called "trading rights" of business firms. In China, only some of the state-owned trading firms have trading rights—that is, the right to engage in imports and exports. These rights are not granted to VTEs, private businesses, and foreign-invested enterprises. In recent years, the Chinese government has started to extend trade rights to a limited number of foreign business but not yet to private businesses of Chinese citizens.

Market-Oriented Reform

The power centers and their stakes, effectiveness, and priority concerns are displayed in Table C.1.

Assessing the Chinese Case

In many ways, China is moving away from a centrally planned economy to a more market-oriented economy. The state sector is no longer the dominant player in the Chinese economy, though it is still a key player. Yet the Chinese economy will continue to be troubled by an ailing state enterprise sector and an inefficient banking system. Currently, two-thirds of SOEs are operating in deficits. The banking system is loaded by nonperforming loans to the SOEs, which account for more than one-fifth of its total assets. Restructuring the SOEs and recapitalizing the banking system would impose heavy costs on the economy and drag down growth.

Other problems include the decline of the fiscal strength of the central government. Government revenue relative to GDP has been declining, and there has been a rising public-sector deficit. In addition, the rising inequality in distribution of income and the regional disparity in level of economic development between the eastern coastal region and the middle and western regions may affect Chinese economic growth one way or another.

The Chinese government has realized the crucial importance of the SOE reform. Its strategy will be the so-called *zhua da, fang xiao*, or "grasp the big, let go the small," thus focusing on transforming the top 1,000 firms into "the pillar of the national economy," while leaving the remaining 117,000 medium and small SOEs to be merged with other SOEs, taken over by private or foreign firms, or go bankrupt.

Despite China's seriousness in reforming SOEs, its broader industrial direction remains unclear, perhaps yet to be decided. Will it try to build its own multinationals, whether these are like the western-type multinationals, Japanese *keiretsu*, or the Korean *chaebol* system? Its economy may be fashioned with pieces of all three models. In all three, the firms are privately owned, yet Chinese conglomerates will remain under effective government control as the state holds the largest stake in them. The *chaebols* are still the dominant player in the Korean

Table C.1

Chinese CPCs and the Policy Space

		Monetary Policy	Fiscal Policy		Trade Policy	Market-Oriented Reform
		Credit Policy	Government Spending	Fiscal Federalism	Access to WTO	Rule of Law and Market Disciplines
PLA-Related Enterprises	Aim	A loose credit policy	Increasing government spending on defense and defense industries	Unclear, regional armies may prefer a decentralized government, while a strong central government could increase military spending	Against major concession	Against clearly defined legal rules and market disciplines
	Channel	COSTIND, military and political leadership	COSTIND, military and political leadership	Central and regional military and political leadership	COSTIND, military and political leadership	COSTIND
	Effectiveness	2	3	2	2	3
	Dynamic	Down	Up	Down	Down	Down
Princelings' Enterprises	Aim	A loose credit policy	Increasing government spending, especially investment spending	Unclear, some prefer a strong central government, while some others prefer a decentralized system	Against major concession and market opening	Strongly against clearly defined legal rules and market disciplines
	Channel	Political leadership	Political leadership	Political leadership	Political leadership	Political leadership
	Effectiveness	3	2	3	1	3
	Dynamic	Down	Down	Down	Down	Down

Table C.1—Continued

		Monetary Policy	Fiscal Policy		Trade Policy	Market-Oriented Reform
		Credit Policy	Government Spending	Fiscal Federalism	Access to WTO	Rule of Law and Market Disciplines
State-Owned Enterprises	Aim	A loose credit policy	Increasing government spending, especially subsidies to SOEs and fixed investment	A fiscally strong central government	Strongly against major concessions in subsidies to SOEs and significant market opening	Against clearly defined legal rules and market disciplines
	Channel	Ministries of industries	Ministries of industries	Ministries of industries	Ministries of industries	Ministries of industries
	Effectiveness	4	3	2	4	3
	Dynamic	Down	Down	Down	Down	Down
Village And Township Enterprises	Aim	A loose credit policy	Increasing provincial and local government spending, but not central government spending and subsidies	A decentralized fiscal system	Against major concessions on market access, welcome trading rights	Support clearly defined legal rules and market disciplines
	Channel	Provincial and local governments	Provincial and local governments	Provincial and local governments	Provincial and local governments	Unclear
	Effectiveness	3	3	3	3	3
	Dynamic	Up	Up	Up	Up	Up

Table C.1—Continued

		Monetary Policy	Fiscal Policy		Trade Policy	Market-Oriented Reform
		Credit Policy	Government Spending	Fiscal Federalism	Access to WTO	Rule of Law and Market Disciplines
Private Enterprises	Aim	May prefer a loose credit policy	Increasing government spending on infrastructure, but not on subsidies	Indifferent	Welcome trading rights and market opening measures	Strongly support clearly defined legal rules and market disciplines
	Channel	Federation of Industry and Commerce (FIC) and other associations of private business	FIC and other associations for private business		FIC and other associations for private business	FIC and other associations of business
	Effectiveness	2	1		1	2
	Dynamic	Up	Down		Up	Up
Foreign Invested Enterprises	Aim	May prefer a loose credit policy	Increasing government spending on infrastructure, but not on subsidies	Indifferent	Strongly support major concessions and market opening	Strongly support clearly defined legal rules and market disciplines
	Channel	*Quanxi* with government leadership, central and local governments	*Quanxi* with government leadership, central and local governments		*Quanxi* with government leadership, central and local governments	*Quanxi* with government leadership
	Effectiveness	2	2		4	3
	Dynamic	Up	Up		Up	Up

NOTES: The effectiveness scale ranges from minimum effectiveness (1) to highly effective (5). The scoring is based on judgments after careful and comparative reviews of the influences of CPCs appearing on the text. Shaded areas represents areas of high interests.

economy (the top ten chaebol account for around two-thirds of the Korean economy), while in China, the state sector already has declined to less than a third of the economy. And the *chaebol* system has already revealed its limitations since the collapse of the Hanbo—one of the Korean *chaebol*.

China has been moving toward a more market-oriented and open economy, and this trend is likely to continue in the post-Deng period, as is the relative decline in the influence of traditional power centers and the rising influence of the new ones, despite the government's intention to remain in control. Yet China still has a long way to go. A well-functioning market economy requires clearly defined property rights and rules of law, which are lacking in China. China's emerging business culture can be portrayed most clearly by summing up across the various policy spaces—monetary, fiscal, trade, and more general market-oriented reform. Doing that will also display the stakes of the power centers and the balance of power among them.

With regard to the monetary policy space, inflationary pressure came from excessive monetary growth, which was attributed to higher-than-expected investment spending by the SOEs, the lack of budgetary restraint by the state sector, large increase in wages for government employees, and the increase in payments to farmers. The major monetary policy tool to control inflation is credit control. Stringency in controlling credit would be felt most directly and strongly by the SOEs, as many of them rely on state banks' credit to survive. VTEs would also be affected because it would be difficult for local governments to obtain loans for them under the central government's tightened control on the money supply. However, private enterprises and foreign-invested enterprises would be less affected by credit-control policy because they rely much less on state bank loans as a source of capital.

That said, SOEs, including PLA-related and *taizidang* enterprises, may still have the highest leverage in monetary policy among the power centers. Although the share of the state sector in the Chinese economy is gradually declining, the SOEs still support much of the nation's social security system, including employment, housing, and health care. The government continues to feed loss-making SOEs and does not want them to go bankrupt for fear of causing massive unemployment and so risking social and political instability. Whenever the tightening of credit leads to the risks of large-scale bankruptcy among SOEs, the pressure to loosen control over credit becomes formidable. This explains the relaxation of credit in the late spring and summer of 1994.

In fiscal policy, among the power centers, SOEs would strongly prefer expansion, with higher levels of government spending. By contrast, while other power centers, such as VTEs, foreign-invested enterprises (FIEs), and private enterprises, may support government spending on infrastructure, from which they would benefit, they oppose government spending on SOEs, with which they compete, and are definitely against government subsidies to state enterprises.

Among the power centers, SOEs would support the strengthening of the central government's fiscal position, but VTEs as a group would be strongly against it. Other power centers, including FIEs and private enterprises, would not be affected significantly by such policy changes. The other tax issue is the cancellation of preferential tax treatment to FIEs, a change welcomed by all power centers except FIEs.

In the trade area, SOEs would be most affected if China accepted the conditions set by the United States and other members for entering the WTO. SOEs, including those that are PLA-related and *taizidang*-related, receive subsidies and enjoy preferential access to government investment, both of which are against WTO rules. In addition, SOEs control the strategic sectors of the economy, which are protected by high tariff and non-tariff barriers. VTEs would also be affected because they benefit from protected domestic markets. Although private enterprises will also be affected by market-opening measures, the benefits from the rule of law and trading rights governed by WTO regulations would outweigh the loss. Foreign-invested enterprises would benefit most from China's trade liberalization measures, as required by WTO membership.

If influence in trade policy is ranked according to share in China's exports, VTEs would be most influential, followed by FIEs, SOEs, PLA-related, *taizidang* enterprises, and private business.

Finally, the broader question of market reform will require the transformation of SOEs, including their privatization. It will also necessitate improved rules for governing markets, along with visible means for enforcing those rules. This package of measures would not be welcomed by SOEs, PLA-related enterprises, and princelings. SOEs could only be transformed by letting a significant proportion go bankrupt. Moreover, a market governed by the rule of law would mean a level playing field for all players, diminishing the special status enjoyed by the military or political leadership, as well as state enterprises. However, these policies would be strongly supported by FIEs and the private sector, as they will clearly benefit from a well-functioning market system.

Overall, with the decline of the state sector and the passing away of the old generation leaders, the influence of SOEs and political-leadership related power centers is declining over time. The influence of the PLA-related power centers is not quite clear. On the one hand, the role of the military in Chinese government decisionmaking is increasing, which would increase its influence in economic policy; on the other hand, market-oriented reform would undermine its leverages on a number of policy issues. With the rapid expansion of VTEs, private business, and foreign investment, these power centers can be expected to play larger roles in Chinese economic policymaking in the future.

D. Evidence from the Cases: Indonesia

Indonesia, like many other emerging markets, is a country in transition. After two decades (1966–1986) of rapid economic development and change, the country has been attempting for over a decade to implement what might be called "market reforms"—expanding the role of the private sector by deregulating the economy and shrinking subsidies to SOEs and opening the economy to foreign competition. The process is producing winners and losers as it alters the rules of the economic game and thus changes the balance of power in domestic politics—in particular, the respective roles played by the state and nonstate economic actors.

Older frames of reference for understanding Indonesia—an authoritarian regime in which the depoliticization of civil society has been pushed to the extreme under Suharto's regime—are less relevant after over a decade (since 1986) of profound deregulation and internationalization of the economy. Policymaking and policies are becoming less the exclusive purview of governments and more the outcome of a complex process in which diverse groups participate, with varying degrees of influence. In a seminal book on a changing Indonesia, Andrew MacIntyre reviewed specific actions taken by nonstate actors (business associations) in three industries and concluded that the "widely shared view [that] political life in Indonesia is overwhelmingly dominated by the state, with policymaking processes being subject to tight control" is no longer satisfactory after two decades (research was carried out in 1986-1987) of rapid economic development.[1]

MacIntyre's analysis was at the industry level and, as such, very detailed and precise in its assessment of the interests at stake and the determination of winners and losers. Our report analyzes change in Indonesia at a higher level of aggregation and uses CPCs as the unit of analysis.

CPC Analysis

We review Indonesia's CPCs in the following order: Sino-Indonesians, SOEs, Suharto and kin, and the foreign sector. The order is consistent with a subjective

---

[1]Andrew MacIntyre, *Business and Politics in Indonesia*, Singapore and Australia: Allen & Unwin, 1992, p. vii.

ranking of the CPCs, which takes into consideration the size of the CPC, its ability to influence policy, and its vulnerability to policy changes. We rank the Sino-Indonesian conglomerates first because they hold by far the greatest raw power among CPCs, commanding probably 70 percent of all private activities in Indonesia and dominating the fastest-growing sectors of the economy. These conglomerates are mostly the product of the New Order (Suharto's regime since 1966). They were considered the beneficiaries of regulation in the 1970s (i.e., protectionism and subsidized credits) and are considered today the beneficiaries of the deregulation and the opening of Indonesia since the mid-1980s. Their power is quite precarious because of the high vulnerability of both Sino-Indonesians' position in Indonesia and their heavy reliance on personal channels of influence to see their policy choices adopted. Their power is thus highly dependent on the continuation of Suharto's New Order.

We have ranked SOEs second because of their share of the economy and their ability to foster or block policies. They have thrived for the past three decades (until 1997) thanks in large part to protection they received from the technical ministries that oversee them. The record of the past three decades suggests that their vulnerability to changes in economic policy is very low. However, one of the key decisions of the package of reform measures agreed upon between the Indonesian government and the IMF in October and November 1997 is the transfer of control of SOEs from the line ministries, back to the Ministry of Finance. The influence of SOEs will be greatly reduced by this one action, but bureaucratic stonewalling will remain an important tool at the disposal of the line ministries and the SOEs they used to supervise.

Although SOEs are retarding economic growth and development because of their low levels of efficiency and the large share of the economy they occupy, they are an essential part of the Indonesian economy. The political imperative to have a counterweight to Sino-Indonesian power makes it necessary to have a commanding state sector. The Achilles' heel of the SOEs is that they are virtually absent from or losing ground to private competition in the two fastest-growing sectors in the Indonesian economy, the very sectors dominated by Sino-Indonesians: manufacturing exports and banking. Therefore, the SOEs' share of the economy is set to decline inexorably. Thus, overall, the SOEs constitute a large, powerful, but weakening CPC.

The third CPC in our ranking is that of the Suharto family. The gap in size and scope, if not influence, between the first two CPCs and the other two is immense. Although the family represents the second-fastest growing CPC (after Sino-Indonesians), the total revenues of Suharto-related businesses in 1995 represented only 23.2 percent of the largest Sino-Indonesian conglomerate

(Salim), or 2.3 percent of GDP. Given its access to the president, this CPC has tremendous influence relative to its small size, and its development is crucial to Indonesia's development of a successful *pribumi* sector (*pribumi* being indigenous Indonesians, i.e., non–ethnic Chinese). The post-1986 institutionalization of the family's activities and the public listing of its companies have contributed to a decreased vulnerability to political change. Yet, its obvious close connection to the presidential palace (and reliance on "special deals" to further its business interests) remains an important liability because of the popular resentment its wealth generates. The recent crisis in Indonesia has highlighted this vulnerability.

Finally, the fourth CPC is the group of enterprises controlled by foreigners. Their economic power is still very limited, except in the energy (oil & gas, and mining) sector. Direct investment by foreign firms was less than 2 percent of GDP from 1990 through 1995, while its share of gross capital formation was below 4 percent but rising.[2] Because the interests of this CPC are largely congruent with the policies advocated by large international organizations (e.g., IMF, World Bank) or western governments (e.g., U.S., Japan, or EU), its interests are well defended, especially in times of crisis, at the highest levels of the Indonesian government. They remain, however, highly vulnerable to changes in trade and investment regulations.

In addition to these four CPCs, we also address the possibility of including the military or the group of *pribumi* entrepreneurs and businesses as a CPC. The role of the military is so central in Indonesia that it would not be appropriate to evaluate power centers without considering this organization. Had this analysis taken place in the first decade of Indonesia's New Order, the military would have been a CPC because it had direct commercial activities. This has changed; although the military still is probably the most important power center in Indonesia, its limited direct interest in commercial matters does not warrant its consideration as a CPC.

Finally, we assess whether to include *pribumi* businesses as a CPC. We do not consider them as a separate CPC for three reasons. First, the aggregate size of this group of firms (less than 15 percent of private industry) is still too small to be considered a separate CPC. Second, the average size of the *pribumi* firms does not allow them to influence policy in any significant manner, except through rare but sometimes successful collective action (e.g., MacIntyre's examples). Third, *pribumi* businesses are mostly in engineering and construction, because most of

---

[2]Hal Hill, *The Indonesian Economy Since 1966: Southeast Asia's Emerging Giant,* Hong Kong: Cambridge University Press, 1996, Figure 5.4, p. 77.

them got their start through government contracts to build infrastructure during the latter years of the oil boom. Although this situation has changed over recent years, the breadth of *pribumi* businesses cannot be compared to that of the Sino-Indonesians.

Policy Analysis

The four policy issues under consideration are (1) monetary policy (strict banking supervision), (2) fiscal policy (SOE reform), (3) trade liberalization, and (4) investment policy (equal treatment of foreign investors).

The Indonesian banking sector was greatly deregulated, first in June 1983 and then in October 1988. Since then, open-market operations and control of bank reserves are used instead of direct control of credit. The consequence of this liberalization of the banking industry has been an explosion of private banks and the retreat of state-owned banks as main financial intermediaries. Deregulation has turned, in some cases, into no regulation or supervision. Important rules regulating the health of the banking sector have not been enforced by the central bank. For example, rules regarding bank reserve requirements, rules limiting lending to a single borrower, or rules limiting lending to shareholders (of the bank) were flaunted by many small private banks.

In the wake of the financial crisis of summer and fall 1997, a large part of the banking sector was in trouble, and some banks were virtually bankrupt. On November 1, 1997, the first concrete action of the Indonesian government after reaching agreement with the IMF was to close 16 insolvent banks. In addition to the closing of insolvent banks, weak banks are required to present a financial plan to Bank Indonesia explaining how they will deal with their weak position.

In December 1986, following the abrupt drop in oil revenues, President Suharto called for an assessment of the financial soundness of every SOE and requested that a program be developed for their restructuring, including the possibility of selective privatization. The pace of privatization has been very slow, despite the president's direct interest in the matter. This is revealing of the power of SOEs and the bureaucracy to stonewall policies that they oppose. In addition to this resistance, implementation problems (how to sell state assets to whom) have contributed to this slow progress. Progress has been made on the "how" issue with the modernization of Indonesia's financial sector. The issue of "to whom" to sell (assuming availability of funds and willingness to invest) remains political dynamite. It remains politically impossible to raise the share of any of the potential buyers—Sino-Indonesians, Suharto's relatives, or foreign firms—and no other source of capital exists. Privatization will accelerate, but the interests of the

CPCs, coupled with the realities of Indonesia's tense ethnic and social tensions, will keep this effort from turning into a "big bang" privatization process.

Although Indonesia has already come a long way from the system of import license and export requirements in place until 1986, it still has a substantial amount of trade subjected to high tariffs or to NTBs. Since May 1986, the Indonesian government unveils each year a new list of tariff and NTB reductions. Also, the Uruguay round of the worldwide General Agreement on Tariffs and Trade (GATT) led to drastic tariff cuts in basic industries. Despite these important steps in the direction of freer trade, some sectors remain stubbornly protected, and tariffs or NTBs directly targeted at particular goods still exist. In most cases, the protection can be linked quite directly to powerful domestic interest, either to SOEs or to private conglomerates (Sino-Indonesian and/or Suharto and kin).

Since 1986, although private investment has been replacing the public sector as the main provider of investment funds, domestic investment does not suffice to meet the five-year plan's growth objectives. Foreign investment is also needed. Although the share of foreign investment (relative to domestic private investment) has been steadily falling, foreign investment remains necessary for Indonesia, not only in quantity but also in quality (with the know-how that foreign firms bring with them). Just as a small party in a government coalition can have disproportionate influence, foreign investment commands influence disproportionate to its size and is keenly wooed. Despite numerous investment deregulation packages over the last decade, investment controls remain extremely complex and too decentralized (involving too many different government agencies and ministries).

CPC Interests and Public Policies

The position of CPCs regarding strict banking supervision can be summarized as follows. The foreign and SOE CPCs stand to gain from the policy but for different reasons. SOEs look favorably at stricter banking supervision because it affects mostly private banks and not state-owned banks. As long as the private banking sector is in transition, not to say turmoil, the Indonesian government will continue to hold its deposits in state-owned banks. In the longer term, however, a more-efficient private banking sector will be more of a threat to state-owned banks than they are today. Yet, SOEs have little leverage on banking regulation (which is decided by the central bank and the president's key economic advisors). The foreign sector also stands to benefit from a healthier banking system, because foreign banks can better compete in a level playing field and because foreign firms probably appreciate doing business with efficient banks. The foreign sector has no leverage on this issue, except with the help of the IMF.

In contrast, the two other CPCs—Sino-Indonesian conglomerates and Suharto and kin—stand to lose if Bank Indonesia continues to close insolvent banks and tighten supervision regulations. Suharto and relatives face more adversarial effects than the Sino-Indonesian conglomerates because they do not have the "deep pockets" of the latter. Both CPCs have fairly high leverage on this policy because of their close connections to the presidential palace. Such leverage is limited, however, by the fact that monetary policy has historically been the purview of a small group of technical experts whom the president trusts over and above his closest friends.

SOE Privatization

Unsurprisingly, the SOEs are the staunchest opponents of SOE privatization. The transfer of authority over them back to the Finance Ministry should greatly deflect SOEs' ability to oppose privatization efforts. Suharto's kin and the foreign sector both would be positively affected by an increased pace of privatization, but because of their connections to the president, the kin have more leverage. The purchase of assets from SOEs is the fastest way for Suharto's kin to expand their business empires. Yet, given the popular resentment against their fast growing business empires, their massive purchase of government-owned assets is politically unacceptable. For the foreign sector as well, acquisition of SOEs' assets is a good way to get a foothold or expand business in Indonesia. Yet, economic nationalism in the political discourse is still very much alive, and senior policymakers do not want to rely too much on foreign capital.

The Sino-Indonesians have very mixed feelings about privatization. On the one hand, from a business perspective, they are keenly interested in privatization. From a political standpoint, they are reluctant to acquire SOEs' assets, because they fear a political backlash against their increased control over national production. Sino-Indonesians have more diversification and growth strategies available (other than acquisition of existing companies) than conglomerates controlled by Suharto's kin or foreign firms. On balance, they probably prefer a slower privatization process, which their conglomerates could more easily "digest" without popular uproar.

Trade Liberalization

SOEs are generally against trade opening as it undermines their control of the economy. Sino-Indonesian conglomerates and Suharto and kin are in favor of trade liberalization, as a principle; but they are still asking for selective protection for their own projects. Finally, foreign firms are in favor of freer trade and more transparency in trade regulations. In terms of leverage, it is evident that the CPC with the least leverage, in normal times, is the foreign sector. Yet, in times of crisis, pressure from foreign governments, relayed through the IMF can yield substantial changes in policy that would not otherwise have taken place. These changes, by leveling the playing field, are to the advantage of competitive foreign firms, and, in time, of Indonesian consumers.

Foreign Investment

The Sino-Indonesians, Suharto and kin, and foreign CPCs are in favor of investment reform and a more transparent approval process. Yet, domestic CPCs are still keen on keeping the investment process nontransparent, because this allows them to extract economic rent more easily than can foreign investors who do not know all the ropes of the trade. More investment deregulation means more competition, which is not to the liking of established rent-seekers. SOEs are presumably opposed to investment deregulation, because reform would ultimately decrease the power of the bureaucracy. No evidence, however, was found suggesting that SOEs faced an easier investment approval process than their private domestic counterparts. The foreign firms are strongly in favor of further deregulation and unconditional national treatment.

Indonesian Policy Space

Table D.1 is a policy matrix that articulates the interests of CPCs with the policy issues addressed in the report. Each cell (1) shows the position of a given CPC with respect to a given policy, (2) identifies the channels of influence used to foster that position, (3) assesses the CPC's effectiveness in achieving its goals, and (4) assesses the dynamics of influence (increasing or receding) of the CPC on that particular policy.

Table D.1

Indonesian CPCs and the Policy Space

		Macroeconomic Policy		
		Monetary—Banking Supervision	Fiscal—SOE Reform	Trade Liberalization	Investment Reform
Sino-Indonesian	Aim	Loose supervision	Selective privatization	Selective liberalization	Simplify system
	Channel	President & executive	President & private partners	President & private partners	President & executive
	Effectiveness	Limited	High	High	Limited
	Dynamics	Stable	Increasing	Increasing	Stable
SOE	Aim	Strict supervision	Against privatization	Keep protection	Keep complex system
	Channel	Executive	Executive & private partners	Executive & private partners	Executive &BKPM
	Effectiveness	Limited	High	Limited	Limited
	Dynamics	Receding	Stable	Stable	Stable
Suharto & Kin	Aim	Loose supervision	Selective privatization	Selective liberalization	Simplify system
	Channel	President	President & private partners	President & private partners	President
	Effectiveness	Limited	High	High	Limited
	Dynamics	Stable	Increasing	Increasing	Stable
Foreign	Aim	Strict supervision	Selective privatization	Full-blown liberalization	Simplify system
	Channel	President or stop investing	President or stop investing	President or stop investing	President or stop investing
	Effectiveness	Limited	High	High	Limited
	Dynamics	Increasing	Increasing	Increasing	Increasing

NOTE: Shading indicates items of greatest priority.